TCM
UNDERGROUND

Shirō (Shigeru Amachi) struggles to save the ones he loves in the hell of *Jigoku*.

TCM
UNDERGROUND

50 MUST-SEE FILMS FROM
THE WORLD OF CLASSIC CULT AND
LATE-NIGHT CINEMA

MILLIE DE CHIRICO and **QUATOYIAH MURRY**

Foreword by PATTON OSWALT

RUNNING PRESS
PHILADELPHIA

To my mom, dad, and sister, Faye, Paul, and Stephanie—
thank you for always accepting me exactly as I am.

—MILLIE DE CHIRICO

To my Mom; Daviorr, who is the best big brother and my
biggest cheerleader; and all the angels in my life that I
call friends, who have stuck by my side and supported
me for all these years.

—QUATOYIAH MURRY

Running Press
Hachette Book Group
1290 Avenue of the Americas, New York, NY 10104
www.runningpress.com
@Running_Press

Printed in Italy

First Edition: October 2022

Published by Running Press, an imprint of Perseus
Books, LLC, a subsidiary of Hachette Book Group, Inc.
The Running Press name and logo are trademarks of
the Hachette Book Group.

The Hachette Speakers Bureau provides a wide range
of authors for speaking events. To find out more,
go to www.hachettespeakersbureau.com or call
(866) 376-6591.

The publisher is not responsible for websites (or their
content) that are not owned by the publisher.

Photography credits: pages 17, 46, 47, 62, 64, 65,
68, 69, 70, 90, and 106 courtesy mptv. These images
from the Independent Visions Archive are exclusively
represented by mptv. For more information regarding
licensing or purchasing images from mptv, please
contact mptvimages at www.mptvimages.com.
Courtesy Photofest: pages 83, 84, 123, 125, and 187
Page 144: San Francisco Chronicle/Hearst Newspapers
via Getty Images
All other photos courtesy Turner Classic Movies.

Print book cover and interior design by Josh McDonnell.

Library of Congress Control Number: 2022933405

ISBNs: 978-0-7624-8000-5 (paperback),
978-0-7624-8001-2 (ebook)

Elco

10 9 8 7 6 5 4 3 2 1

CONTENTS

FOREWORD

By PATTON OSWALT

I mean, *any* movie that's beloved is a cult movie, isn't it?

Any movie that punches through the fog of worry, distraction, and ego that we're stuck in creates a cult, even if it's a cult with one adherent. Any work of art that can take us out of—what, ourselves? the world?—is by default creating a tiny space of worship and adulation: where we find our own totems, fetishes, and idols; where we run through comforting rituals. A line of perfectly delivered dialogue is a psalm. An out-of-context image becomes a votive, and plot points and props become liturgical call-and-responses and holy relics.

Or, in less high-minded language, *we dig on that shit over and over again.* And it's a mind-space we can hop into when we're bored or stressed or lonely or can't-even-articulate-how-goddamned-disappointing-reality-is-sometimes fed up.

It's no wonder that Sal Piro, who formed the now decades-strong *Rocky Horror Picture Show* midnight movie cult, was a former seminary student. Into a dark space full of strangers, past the stroke of midnight when you felt the zombie-thrill of being alive and awake while the world was asleep, marched the first wave of cult films: *Eraserhead* and *El Topo*, *Pink Flamingos* and *The Harder They Come*, *Harold and Maude* and *Night of the Living Dead*. Forbidden twilight pleasures that built an audience before Twitter or Instagram, before texting and flash mobs. Unkillable viral visions that gathered weekly crowds or, as Ben Barenholtz famously said about *Eraserhead*—"Only forty people a week go see this thing, but it's the *same forty people.*"

But like all outré, fringe, or outsider pleasures, these were soon absorbed into the mainstream. Divine eats a dog turd at the end of *Pink Flamingos*. Twenty years later, Austen Powers drinks a mug of shit in the first reel of *The Spy Who Shagged Me*. David Lynch makes prime-time TV shows and Chanel No. 5 ads. And zombies, zombies, zombies everywhere.

Where are the new cult films coming from?

I can't answer that in the short space I have here. You could argue that viral videos are the new cult movies for our blip-span age of attention. Online memes are the new samizdat. Certainly the impulse to create new cult films hasn't gone away. I can remember going to midnight screenings of *Showgirls*, where patrons were desperately, clumsily trying to *force* a cult into being, through sheer will and lungpower. But no matter how much brown rice and vegetables they threw at the screen, it didn't take hold.

It can't be forced. It has to . . . just . . . happen. It has to happen before the audience or the film or reality itself realizes it's happened. And then there's a point when it's too late, when you're looking back and the audience is waiting for the little moments that burrowed into their heads, that stayed with them, and no one can pinpoint the exact moment when a roomful of strangers began speaking a secret code language. Part of the power of cult films is being content with never being able to reverse-engineer the beginning. It's not *about* the beginning—it's about what the connections ends up being—as if they were there all along.

If Millie De Chirico and Quatoyiah Murry had just listed the fifty new cult films they've selected for this book then it'd be a useless endeavor. We're all waist-deep in lists, as nostalgia threatens to consume any forward motion—in culture, in arts, in human progress.

But what the authors have done here, and what's so amazing, is how they've captured the feeling of being captured by a film cult. Especially the little sidebars, the "Spotlight on . . ." and "OMG Moment" highlights. There they are, in plain daylight—the icons and the rituals.

Some actors and actresses—for Michael J. Weldon, of the immortal *Psychotronic Encyclopedia of Film*, it was Vincent Price and Bela Lugosi—become their own *genre* of film, through sheer personality, life force, and quirkiness. Right from the get-go Yaphet Kotto is recognized as one of these (literally, the man was a giant) towering figures, that create their own spaces on celluloid where cultists can pay their respects. Other performers who get this (much-deserved) spotlight are Antonio Fargas, Susan Tyrrell (Academy Award–nominated!), Paul Bartel, Mary Woronov, and the immortal Shirley Stoler. There are others. There will be others. There will always be those figures who are bigger than the films they're in, even if they're only on-screen for a minute. I happen to worship at the altar of Michael Ripper, a bit player in Hammer Films who you *can't not watch* (look him up). Oh, sorry, I'm supposed to be writing this foreword, not going off on a tangent. But that's the life of a cultist.

And the "OMG Moment" sidebars. Yes yes yes. These are those scenes, sequences, or mere seconds of screen time which become nexus points for a film cult's worship. Monster sex in *Possession*, the descent into hell in *Jigoku*, the McDonald's commercial in *Mac & Me*. They also acknowledge those scenes where OMG becomes WTF, especially in the case of *The Brood*, *The House by the Cemetery*, and *House*. The bar needs to be set somewhere.

Don't read this book from the beginning. Flip around, stop where it grabs you, let it lead you backward and forward and sideways. That's how you should watch and rewatch and remember movies, anyway. Moment and feeling always conquer plot and logic, especially out beyond the edge.

Here you go!

—**PATTON OSWALT**
Los Angeles, 2022

INTRODUCTION

As two women with a lifelong appreciation for movies often considered "bad" or "weird" by mainstream standards, we never imagined we'd one day be writing a book about what some might call our "peculiar" taste in film. Growing up with a passion for outsider art and other dark corners of popular culture, our awareness of cult movies came from many different places: late-night cable television series such as *Night Flight* and *Up All Night*, recommendations from older siblings or video-store clerks, bootleg VHS tapes from friends, midnight screenings and movie nights in someone's dorm room, and the dog-eared pages of such film reference books as *Cult Movies* and *The Psychotronic Video Guide*. The films we discovered over the years had either slipped through the cracks of availability or had been deemed unremarkable and unwatchable by critics as well as by general audiences, judging by box-office receipts. Nevertheless, we've always gravitated toward subversive cinema, finding something special and endearing in each cult movie we came upon, enough to want to keep their legacies alive regardless of how unfortunately judged or forgotten they've been.

As part of an ethos that all movies deserve a chance to be seen, Turner Classic Movies launched TCM Underground on the Friday night before Halloween in 2006, as a showcase for cult films. The franchise was initially conceived by Eric Weber, a former TCM marketer and fellow cult movie lover. The idea of it being a place for cult cinema that lived outside of "normal" TCM hours was in the spirit of what got us into these films in the first place. Those of us who work on TCM Underground believe that being a well-rounded cinephile means having a willingness to be open to viewing anything and everything (and we mean *anything*). Over the years, TCM Underground has shown a varied assortment of cult titles, sometimes leaning toward the "canon" made by well-established directors like David Cronenberg or John Waters, and sometimes giving a spotlight to renegade filmmakers who are virtually unknown in Hollywood.

Out of the more than four hundred films that have aired in TCM Underground's history, it was hard to come up with just fifty to write about for this book. We did not set out to create a definitive list of the "Best" or "All-Time Greatest" cult films; that seemed like a futile endeavor. Instead, we selected films that had the biggest impact on us, ones that we felt needed a spotlight, ones that represented the rich diversity missing from mainstream films of the era, and ones that would exemplify the scope of what TCM Underground has to offer. We (Millie, TCM Underground programmer, and Quatoyiah, former TCM editorial manager) split the fifty titles between us, so while reading you'll hear Toyiah's passionate plea for the Blaxploitation parody *I'm Gonna Git You Sucka* and also understand her unsettling desire to learn the choreography from that McDonald's dance sequence in *Mac and Me*; or learn about Millie's fascination with the deeply strange 1970s melodrama *The Baby*, as well as her thoughts on the randomness of seeing two people kissing on top of a dumpster during the opening sequence of *Roller Boogie*. We dive into our favorite microgenres, like Canuxploitation, Sexploitation, and Grande Dame Guignol, and we gush about our cult movie heroes such as Pam Grier, Paul Bartel, Mary Woronov, and William Castle. Be it stoners, skaters, stalkers, or prank callers—we cover so much ground that it's likely all your niche preferences are covered among our various picks. Some of these films will be easier to find than others, and we encourage you to seek out physical media (don't forget your local library!) as well as the multitude of streaming options that are currently available. Even finding photos to illustrate these pages was a challenge in some instances, given the low-budget history of the movies featured, but we did the best we could to offer visuals of some of filmdom's weirdest moments.

Revisiting these movies was an absolute delight for the two of us and was an amazing reminder of how special the art of cinema really is. We urge you to have fun (and keep an open mind!) in both reading about and viewing our selections, and we hope some will end up being favorites of yours, too. And when late-night Friday rolls around, keep your TV tuned to TCM Underground for more of the most offbeat, strange, and downright deranged offerings in cinema history.

IT'S
CRIME
TIME

Stories of murder, theft, and other forms of lawbreaking have been a fascination of film lovers since the early days of cinema. This next group of titles are some of our all-time favorite cult movies about what can happen in the quest for law and order. From the intense cat-and-mouse game between a thief and his victim in the Canadian thriller *The Silent Partner* to the investigation of a mafia-involved heist in Harlem that drives the gritty, urban crime film *Across 110th Street*, these movies pull no punches when it comes to showing the darker side of life.

ACROSS 110TH STREET

USA, 1972 • COLOR, 102 MINUTES

Frank Mattelli (Anthony Quinn) goes head-to-head with a Harlem crime boss (Richard Ward).

DIRECTOR: Barry Shear   **SCREENPLAY:** Luther Davis

STARRING: Anthony Quinn (Frank Mattelli), Yaphet Kotto (Lt. Pope),
Paul Benjamin (Jim Harris), Anthony Cannon (Sal), Antonio Fargas (Henry),
Anthony Franciosa (Nick D'Salvio), Paul Harris (Mr. C),
Andrea Frierson (Florence Jessup), Richard Ward (Doc Johnson)

Shortly before the explosion of the Blaxploitation era and the popularity of mob-centric movies in US film markets, this thrilling 1972 crime drama was released and quickly lost in the shuffle. Produced by Mexican-born classic movie star Anthony Quinn, *Across 110th Street* fused several styles within the action genre, then managed to be a forerunner for pivotal crime dramas yet to be released at the time, such as Martin Scorsese's *Mean Streets* (1973) and Sidney Lumet's *Serpico* (1973). Today, *Across 110th Street* is still vastly underrecognized in part due to the timing of its release and also because of its largely Black cast. As indicated by the film's title—a reference to the New York City dividing line that separates the prestigious, bourgeois class of Manhattan from the long-underserved, culturally rich, and predominately Black Harlem—*Across 110th Street* is equally a crime thriller

Antonio Fargas alongside Anthony Franciosa

The streets of 1970s Harlem on full display

rooted in the conventions of its genre and a rare mainstream dissection of how class and bureaucracy have negatively affected largely minority American neighborhoods.

Quinn stars as Frank Mattelli, the haggard, violent captain of Harlem's 27th precinct. After the robbery of a Mafia boss goes wrong—resulting in the murder of two officers, members of the Mafia, and members of a local Black crime syndicate—Mattelli shows up to the aftermath only to learn that he's not the lead on the case. Instead, he must take a back seat to the new lieutenant, Pope (Yaphet Kotto), a Black, college-educated rising detective who plays by the rules. While the two clash as Mattelli's racist, violent, and corrupt ways bubble to the surface during the case, the three robbers' actions spark a domino effect. They each separately plan their escape from Harlem, but unbeknownst to them, the Italian Mafia and the kingpin of the local Black mob are hot on their tails to find the stolen money and make an example of them. The resulting action makes the film a patchwork of genres: heist, procedural drama, and cat-and-mouse chase with a bit of underplayed social commentary, adding rich layers of depth to the city and the players involved.

Actor Paul Benjamin has an intense moment with Maria Carey.

Upon its release, *Across 110th Street* was lambasted by critics, with the *Los Angeles Times* dismissing it as nothing more than a "violence freak's special" while Gene Siskel wrote the film off as being standard fare for the time. However, it's hard to understand that criticism considering the era in which the film was released. It's indeed a brutal film that depicts extreme violence, including torture, but nothing about it is excessive in the manner of a film like *The Godfather*, 1972's biggest hit, or Sam Peckinpah's *The Wild Bunch*, made—and highly praised—a mere three years prior. What makes *Across 110th Street*

feel so much more violent is the creative and immersive way director Barry Shear and cinematographer Jack Priestley capture the action. Shear's decision to shoot on location in Harlem, New York, is likewise responsible, taking viewers inside apartments, brothels, and private spaces of the city in intimate ways. Screenwriter Luther Davis's focus on the ruthless nature of survival and order in urban America lends to an authentic grit of the concrete jungle.

Comparisons to *In the Heat of the Night* (1967) are inevitable due to the racial dynamic at play between Mattelli and Pope. However,

Maria (Maria Carey) makes a call.

here Pope doesn't have anything to prove to Mattelli because of his race in the way *In the Heat of the Night*'s Virgil Tibbs does to Chief Bill Gillespie. Neither is Pope's race a roadblock in the case. His motivation is instead a fair shot to move up the ranks without being corrupted. Quinn's Mattelli, on the other hand, seems to be confronted for the first time with a mirror to his actions and must assess his own demons that he's buried over the years. The dynamic between the two characters is on full display during an intense interrogation scene. Mattelli proudly thinks he's schooling Pope by telling him his method of questioning works for getting answers after bare-fistedly beating a civilian into unconsciousness in the interrogation room. Pope confronts the violent, archaic ways of the captain by calmly reminding him that the battered witness has not provided any answers to his questions and now cannot. This scene feels chilling and ahead of its time, as police brutality against African Americans was just beginning to be discussed in a Richard Nixon–era America.

But it's not just the racial politics between the cops or even their interplay with the mob and their bureaucratic fight for power among Harlem's underworld that makes *Across 110th Street* worthy of renewed attention. It's also the heavy focus on the "villains" at the core of the film: Jim Harris, Sal, and Henry. Although not all three characters are given the same level of depth and development, they are all presented as socially marginalized men desperate for change. Sal works at a laundromat but wants economic freedom, while Henry craves a chance to live a life of luxury. Jim is the soul of the trio, however. Actor Paul Benjamin delivers a gut-wrenching performance in which he vocalizes the reasons for their dangerous decision to rob the mob. Jim and his partners aren't just criminals robbing for the thrill of the chase or wanting to be the area's next top bosses. They are humans struggling to survive the trials and tribulations endured by residents of Harlem in the 1970s. Jim is an ex-con war veteran dealing with a disability, and, as a Black man in America, those three strikes automatically prevent him from earning a living wage. Therefore, he and his girlfriend must rely on dangerous ways to make ends meet, hers being prostitution.

Across 110th Street is not without its dated tropes, but the film feels surprisingly modern fifty years after its release. Shear gives a needed first-person view into the lives of Harlem residents of the 1970s, but neither through slick, clean production nor through a lens of impoverished exploitation. Shear presents life as it was for a neighborhood in a specific time frame; a neighborhood that made do on its own while capitalism ballooned and separated the haves from the have nots. For these reasons, along with Bobby Womack's killer soundtrack and title song, *Across 110th Street* is an important film that deserves another look as a means of investigating the cycle of crime and disenfranchisement in America.

A Spotlight on . . . Antonio Fargas

Antonio Fargas (1946–) will go down in history as the King of Cool Character Actors in cinema. Having made his uncredited debut in Shirley Clarke's *The Cool World* (1963), Fargas has an impressive 135 credits to his name to date. The tall, suave, and charming actor has had a career of bit parts—normally stereotypical roles of pimp, pusher, or user—but he's managed to rise above the typecasting and bring humanity and star power to his performances. You'll see his name in this book again and outside it, as Fargas is featured in a number of classic, must-see films of the 1970s, including *Cleopatra Jones* (1973), *Shaft* (1971), *Foxy Brown* (1974), *Cornbread, Earl and Me* (1975), and *Car Wash* (1976).

FRIDAY FOSTER

USA, 1975 • COLOR, 90 MINUTES

Colt Hawkins (Yaphet Kotto) and Friday Foster herself (Pam Grier)

DIRECTOR: Arthur Marks   **SCREENPLAY:** Orville H. Hampton, Arthur Marks
STARRING: Pam Grier (Friday Foster), Yaphet Kotto (Colt Hawkins), Godfrey
Cambridge (Ford Malotte), Thalmus Rasulala (Blake Tarr), Eartha Kitt (Madame
Rena), Jim Backus (Enos Griffith), Scatman Crothers (Reverend Noble Franklin),
Paul Benjamin (Senator David Lee Hart), Carl Weathers (Yarbro)

Pam Grier reigned as the undisputed queen of 1970s cinema. With her natural charm, beautiful frame that made her a clotheshorse for an array of designers, and acting chops to match, Grier became an emblem of a changing America and a rapidly shifting cinematic landscape. With the Hollywood studio system in decline, independent and low-budget films were the bread and butter of the industry. At first, this movement was led by Black filmmakers who hadn't received the opportunity to try their hands at moviemaking under the rigid restrictions of the white-dominated Hollywood system. Rudy Ray Moore, Gordon Parks, and Melvin Van Peebles led the pack, causing mostly white producers to throw their hats in the ring and churn out quick and dirty pictures for a profit, resulting in the era of Blaxploitation, an idiom that often results in any film starring a Black lead during this era being misclassified as such.

At the center of this genre was the beautiful, bodacious Grier. Exuding confidence, strength, delicacy, and refinement, Grier got to be what Black women often weren't on-screen, and arguably no movie better showcases that than *Friday Foster*. Stepping away from her usual roles as prisoner, prostitute, or revenge-focused civilian, *Friday Foster* casts Grier as a career woman entangled in an assassination plot. The film was based on the short-lived comic strip of the same name, the original cartoon featuring one of the first Black female stars of a comic. In each serial, Friday, a good-natured photographer,

Friday Foster enjoys an intimate moment with billionaire Blake Tarr (Thalmus Rasulala).

Colt Hawkins nabs bad guy Yarbro (Carl Weathers).

gets herself into a world of trouble. The film adaption finds Friday sent on an assignment to photograph the "Black Howard Hughes," a well-known affluent billionaire who is in Los Angeles for the week. While snapping exclusive shots of the tycoon for the magazine *Glance*, she witnesses an assassination attempt by three men, which places Friday dead center in a large conspiracy with a trail of dead bodies in its wake.

Friday Foster marked the final collaboration for Grier and her home studio, American International Pictures, an independent production and distribution company that made low-budget films aimed at attracting teenagers. Grier rose up in rank at AIP from switchboard operator to superstar in six pictures. While this isn't her most iconic role, the film feels like a sea change from her previous work as a sassy, hard-nosed, independent woman. Grier had embodied these elements effortlessly in films such as *Coffy*, *Foxy Brown*, and *Sheba Baby*, but it's fun to see her downplay her action-star roots in *Friday Foster*. Mostly free from the racial stereotypes commonly seen in Blaxploitation fare, Grier's Friday is a simple career girl, vulnerable and scared, but brave in the face of danger as she avenges a friend's death. She's a headstrong woman who wants answers, and she ropes in her friend, private investigator Colt Hawkins (Yaphet Kotto), to help.

Friday feels more rounded than Grier's previous characters. As she tells a lover, "I'm a woman, I'm a photographer, a big sister to a little brother who's really forty. I know what I want. I like dogs, cats, and men. Not in that order. And I'm a Gemini." Friday is undoubtedly a sexually liberated woman who has her kicks while she can and is loyal to those who are loyal to her. At times, Friday's flippant attitude toward monogamy seems like a callback to Ernst Lubitsch's *Design for Living*. Always known for her ability to look stunning in any outfit she wore, Grier is more toned down here. Gone are the splashy fur coats and bathing suits of previous films. In *Friday Foster*, she still stuns but in business casual outfits: button ups, stripes, and blazers, a fall collection that has inspired some of our outfit choices over the years.

Grier is the star of this film, but an ensemble of fantastic actors grace the screen as well. Yaphet Kotto stars alongside Grier as her trusty confidant, slowly but steadily coming close to stealing every scene he's in, even alongside Grier. Carl Weathers is outstanding as a silent but deadly killer who doesn't speak a single word throughout the entire film, but his presence is magnetic and menacing. Scatman Crothers has a small but memorable part as a minister whose church becomes the target of a violent shootout. But of all the fantastic costars and cameos, the biggest ray of light and flair comes in the form of Eartha Kitt as a flamboyant designer who rolls her r's and sneers with that delectable vivacity that only Kitt can bring.

A Spotlight on . . . Yaphet Kotto

Before his name was immortalized in a song by rapper, comedian, and actor Childish Gambino (better known as Donald Glover), Yaphet Kotto (1939–2021) made a career out of being a recognizable though often unsung talent of cinema and television for more than fifty years. The New York City–born actor of Cameroonian descent and Jewish heritage never truly received the accolades he deserved until his death—and what a shame because Kotto was a groundbreaking showman who delivered dynamic performances throughout his career, no matter how small his parts were. Beloved by many for his breakout performance in Ridley Scott's *Alien* (1979), Kotto became a character actor of sorts with a magnetic presence that shined in every role, and he will forever be adored by fans of genre pictures. It's hard to fathom why he didn't become a bigger star, but we're grateful for the roles he left behind, including his debut in the criminally underrated *Nothing but a Man* (1964); his starring role in cult director Larry Cohen's debut film *Bone* (1972); his unforgettable performance as the villains in *Live and Let Die* (1973) and in the Isaac Hayes Blaxploitation thriller *Truck Turner* (1974); his role in Paul Schrader's directorial debut *Blue Collar* (1978); the Arnold Schwarzenegger sci-fi *Running Man* (1987); and in *Freddy's Dead: The Final Nightmare* (1991).

I SAW WHAT YOU DID

USA, 1965 • COLOR AND B&W, 82 MINUTES

Clockwise from top: Sara Lane, Sharyl Locke, and Andi Garrett on the phone

DIRECTOR: William Castle   **SCREENPLAY:** William P. McGivern

STARRING: Joan Crawford (Amy Nelson), John Ireland (Steve Marak), Sara Lane (Kit Austin), Andi Garrett (Libby Mannering), Leif Erickson (Dave Mannering)

When William Castle's *Macabre* was released in 1958, the notorious horror producer/director took out $1,000 life-insurance policies from Lloyd's of London for the audience in case they died of fright during the screening. Nurses stood by in the lobby of the theater as a hearse waited outside to take away the dead bodies. This was Castle's big entry into the world of the movie gimmick, and he would eventually be known in Hollywood as a one-man film marketing department, a cinema carnival barker, enticing viewers with the scares of their lives. When Alfred Hitchcock's *Psycho* arrived two years later and became a smash hit, it could thank techniques perfected by Castle and his screenings. By the time his film *I Saw What You Did* was released in 1965, the publicity pioneer was already nearing the end of his career with many stunts under his belt, including the self-branded Emergo (flying plastic skeletons that soared over the audience), Percepto (electric buzzers rigged under movie theater seats), and Illusion-O (his own version of 3-D). Castle had a plan for *I Saw What You Did* that included installing seat belts into a section of the movie theater for anyone who might feel the need to run away in terror, but these never actually came to fruition.

A few years earlier, the Bette Davis/Joan Crawford horror classic *What Ever Happened to Baby Jane?* was released, resurrecting the careers of both classic Hollywood stars who were by then in middle age. The two continued to appear in thrillers after the fact, ushering in a micro-genre of horror now titled "Grande Dame Guignol" (also called the "Psychobiddy" or "Hagsploitation" film). These movies were primarily mystery or horror vehicles headed by female stars of the classic Hollywood era who were now deemed past their prime, including (but not limited to) Gloria Swanson, Tallulah Bankhead, Olivia de Havilland, Elizabeth Taylor, Ruth Roman, Veronica Lake, and Shelley Winters. In these films, a formula emerged: a woman commits a murder stemming from jealous rage due to a cheating boyfriend or husband (often

Steve Marak (John Ireland) has his Hitchcockian moment.

Wardrobe test for Joan Crawford's Amy Nelson character

much younger), or an inability to compete with a younger woman (sometimes a daughter). Often, the Psychobiddy traps or confines a relative (a big plot point in *Baby Jane*), and there is a general unease about aging (for Bette Davis in *Baby Jane*, this was signified by her insistence on wearing the same clothes and makeup she wore as a child star), which typically makes them resort to desperate and psychotic measures to qain love and understanding.

The absurdity of this concept is the basis for Grande Dame Guignol, and there was likely no bigger star among these films than Joan Crawford. In the years after the success of *What Ever Happened to Baby Jane?*, she teamed with Castle in 1964 for another Psychobiddy classic, *Strait-Jacket*, in which she plays a homicidal mother who competes with her daughter for the attention of her fiancé. Although Crawford only appears in *I Saw What You Did* for a brief period of time, she was touted as its star. The film is mostly centered around two teenage girls, Libby (Andi Garrett) and Kit (Sara Lane), who prank call random strangers they find in the phone book. Alongside Libby's little sister, Tess (Sharyl Locke), they make a fateful call to a man named Steve Marak, whose wife answers the phone and is promptly murdered by Marak after sneaking up on him in the shower (clearly a nod to *Psycho*). As it turns out, the woman was planning on leaving Marak for being a serial philanderer, including a tryst with Crawford's character, Amy, and Marak must hide her body. All of this is unbeknownst to the girls, who later call Steve back and innocuously tease, "I saw what you did, and I know who you are!," which of course, has greater meaning than they could ever have imagined.

Steve Marak is played by the great Canadian American actor John Ireland, who appeared in dozens of movies in his career, one of the most memorable being Cherry Valance from Howard Hawks's *Red River*. Ireland and Crawford had worked together previously, even having an alleged affair ten years earlier while on the set of the film *Queen Bee*. Ireland is menacing as Marak, which makes Libby and Kit's fascination with him as the movie progresses even darker. Simultaneously, Amy begins to suspect Marak of infidelity, and in true Psychobiddy fashion, blackmails him into marrying her. Marak is a murderer of women, however, and it's frightening to see females both young and old vie for his attention without knowing who he really is. While Crawford as the grande dame, desperate for love at any cost, provides some camp elements to the film, the genuine scares come from the notion that these young girls have no idea what they've gotten into with their hapless prank.

It's because of this that *I Saw What You Did* ends up being bleaker than the deceptively breezy opening credits would suggest. Crawford's scenes are always compelling (as are her big, statement necklaces) and the shower murder is surprisingly violent. The film is never as schlocky as Castle's earlier work, relying more on genuine thrills than flying skeletons or buzzing seats. As a spine-tingler in the Grande Dame Guignol tradition, it hits all the marks you would expect, and those who champion this subgenre generally have a sincere appreciation for an icon like Crawford continuing to make films and finding power in playing complicated characters. At first glance, *I Saw What You Did* might seem like a late, forgettable entry for most of the big-name Hollywood talent involved, but it is actually an effectively frightening film worthy of any insurance policy.

Genre-ly Speaking

For more films in the Grande Dame Guignol tradition, check out the following:

What Ever Happened to Baby Jane? (1962)

Dead Ringer (1964)

Strait-Jacket (1964)

Hush . . . Hush, Sweet Charlotte (1964)

The Nanny (1965)

Die! Die! My Darling! (1965)

Berserk (1967)

Whatever Happened to Aunt Alice? (1969)

Whoever Slew Auntie Roo? (1972)

Night Watch (1973)

The Baby (1973)

Butcher, Baker, Nightmare Maker (1983)

Misery (1990)

Ma (2019)

I'M GONNA GIT YOU SUCKA

USA, 1988 • COLOR, 88 MINUTES

Kung Fu Joe (Steve James) has a legendary showdown with a group of cops.

DIRECTOR: Keenen Ivory Wayans **SCREENPLAY:** Keenen Ivory Wayans

STARRING: Keenen Ivory Wayans (Jack Spade), Bernie Casey (John Slade), Antonio Fargas (Flyguy), Steve James (Kung Fu Joe), Isaac Hayes (Hammer), Jim Brown (Slammer), Ja'net DuBois (Ma Bell), Dawnn Lewis (Cheryl), John Vernon (Mr. Big), Clu Gulager (Lt. Baker), Kadeem Hardison (Willie), Damon Wayans (Leonard)

O f all the films in this book, *I'm Gonna Git You Sucka* is among the few (okay, many) with a special place in our hearts for brilliantly reminiscing on the era of Blaxploitation film, its world of pimps, Black heroes, and fighting against the man, and it does so with one of the funniest scenes in cinematic history, involving a very big platform shoe and a goldfish. Marking the directorial debut of Keenen Ivory Wayans and featuring a recognizable cast of performers, nearly all featured in at least one among this collection of Underground movies, *I'm Gonna Git You Sucka* is the first parody film with a predominately Black cast and one that manages to be less a spoof and more a humorous love letter to a bygone era of films that impacted a generation of moviegoers in the 1970s.

The story centers on Jack Spade, who has recently returned home from the army after discovering that his older brother Junebug has died. A victim of over-gold, or OG'd, Junebug perished from too much gold, leaving behind his worried mother, his widow, Cheryl, and Jack to pick up the pieces. Jack, now hardened by the stresses of war, is determined to find out who is responsible for Junebug's addiction and for turning his neighbors into fiends for expensive gold. Jack's detective work puts him in the crosshairs of a dangerous crime syndicate and jeopardizes the safety of Cheryl and his mother. Jack must enlist the help of the old bloods of the neighborhood to take down that criminal and git that sucka.

Wayans conceived the script after making numerous jokes with friends about tropes in

Bernie Casey, Keenen Ivory Wayans, and Isaac Hayes star as the protagonists.

Blaxploitation movies after having begun his career at the start of the 1980s. The former Tuskegee University engineering student was inspired to try show business after watching Richard Pryor. He made his way from his native Harlem to Hollywood, where he met writer/director Robert Townsend, who encouraged Wayans to become a standup comedian. After succeeding with regular appearances on *The Tonight Show*, Wayans partnered with Townsend to write Townsend's directorial debut, the landmark *Hollywood Shuffle* (1987), in which elements of the duo's prodding at Blaxploitation can be seen during an audition sequence. Wayans went on to

FROM TOP: Isaac Hayes and Jim Brown appear as Hammer and Slammer • Kadeem Hardison on the verge of "OG'ing"

FROM LEFT: Clarence Williams III is a confusing Black Panther member. • Keenen Ivory Wayans behind the scenes

write the opening sketch for Eddie Murphy's *Raw* (1988) before he wrote, directed, and starred in *I'm Gonna Git You Sucka*.

It wasn't easy for Wayans to sell the idea. Initially, studio execs suggested Anthony Michael Hall and Charles Bronson as stars of the picture, but Wayans stuck to his guns and stayed true to the material, bringing an array of beloved icons together for a dazzling ensemble cast, a virtual who's who of Black cinema. With more stars than in heaven, *I'm Gonna Git You Sucka* cements itself as a

historic treasure. Football star and acting superstar Jim Brown, 1970s staple Bernie Casey, and soul singer and star of *Truck Turner* (1974) Isaac Hayes form an iconic trifecta of old-school heroes to lead the film. One would assume that alone is enough to encapsulate the Blaxploitation era, but Wayans worked his magic and brought on more stars.

Five on the Black Hand Side and *Good Times* breakout star Ja'net DuBois easily steals the picture by bringing a deep sincerity and emotional delivery to her role as Jack's lonely and overprotective mother, Ma Bell, with DuBois executing her trademark comedic timing, made even funnier by the absurdity of the film's action and direction. The supporting cast is peppered with equally hilarious and showstopping performers including Antonio Fargas as the obligatory pimp with a wardrobe malfunction, Keenen's younger brother Damon Wayans as a try-hard henchman, Chris Rock as a cheap, swindling restaurant customer, Clarence Williams III as a hypocritical Black power revolutionary, yet another gifted sibling, Kim Wayans, as a hilariously bad nightclub singer, and so many other fantastic comedians and actors who either found fame in the past or would be approaching fame thanks to Wayans's groundbreaking sketch comedy show *In Living Color*, which was still a few years from creation.

The film doesn't require a familiarity with Blaxploitation to make it enjoyable, but this undoubtedly helps, as jokes about the quality of production, the logic of bad guys, and the absurdity of action scenes are painfully side-splitting if you've got a few films of the era under your belt. *I'm Gonna Git You Sucka* was a success in its original release, making double its budget at the box office. The film was set to have a spin-off series centered around Hayes and Brown's characters *Hammer and Slammer*, but the pilot for the series instead became the made-for-TV-movie *Hammer, Slammer & Spade*. Keenen Ivory Wayans's career blossomed and he built a dynasty for his family, all naturally talented in their own right. The influence of *I'm Gonna Git You Sucka* would be felt for decades to come and can be seen in such films as *Undercover Brother* (2002),

Black Dynamite (2009), and the Wayans family vehicles *Don't Be a Menace to South Central While Drinking Your Juice in the Hood* (1996) and the *Scary Movie* franchise.

OMG Moment

Though a cohesive, narrative story, much of *I'm Gonna Git You Sucka* plays out like mini-comedic skits stitched together. Of all the funny moments, from bad fights with obvious stunt doubles to Youth Gang Funday, nothing tops the moment Flyguy is released from prison. An "old head" who went to jail in a time of platform shoes and flashy, bright outfits, Flyguy is released in the unforgivingly cruel world of the late 1980s. Oscar-winning costume designer Ruth E. Carter delivers a career highlight with Flyguy's post-release outfit, complete with the finest accessories only a pimp of extravagant proportions would have, including an impressive pair of platform, aquarian-styled shoes. But the bigger they are, the harder they fall, and Flyguy has a hilarious spill on the streets of Harlem in one of the film's most outrageous scenes.

OPPOSITE, FROM TOP: Antonio Fargas stars as Flyguy. • Blaxploitation legends Bernie Casey, Jim Brown, and Isaac Hayes

THE HARDER THEY COME

JAMAICA, 1972 • COLOR, 120 MINUTES

Jimmy Cliff stars as Ivanhoe Martin.

DIRECTOR: Perry Henzell **SCREENPLAY:** Perry Henzell, Trevor D. Rhone

STARRING: Jimmy Cliff (Ivanhoe "Ivan" Martin), Janet Bartley (Elsa), Carl Bradshaw (Jose Smith), Ras Daniel Hartman (Pedro), Basil Keane (Preacher), Bob Charlton (Hilton), Winston Stona (Detective Ray Jones), Lucia White (Mother)

Credited as the film that "brought reggae to the world," this beloved cult classic from Jamaica was truly a sensation when released. Written and directed by Jamaican natives and starring reggae singer Jimmy Cliff, *The Harder They Come* is loosely based on the real-life crime spree of Vincent Ivanhoe Martin, also known as "Rhyging." A violent criminal with a flair for theatrics, Rhyging (patois for "raging") became a folk hero in Jamaica after his death during a shootout with police in 1948. Like all the most iconic anti-heroes of poverty-stricken eras, Ivan's life was immortalized when director Perry Henzell and playwright Trevor Rhone penned a screenplay about his legacy, updating the story to include relevant aspects of the changing times.

Cliff stars as Ivan, a poor man who has left the rural countryside of Jamaica to live with his estranged mother in Kingston after his grandmother dies. He's turned away without money or prospects, so he aimlessly drifts around the city searching for work and begging for money. Each time, he's met with resistance and hostility until he finally finds passable security singing in a local choir and working for a preacher. Ivan has dreams of being a singer but quickly learns the road to stardom isn't as simple as he thought. After some time, Ivan is finally given the opportunity to prove himself, but he's forced to reckon with the reality that the music industry is just as corrupt as the institutions around him. He's left with little choice but to turn to the drug trade. A bust causes him to kill a police officer, sending him on the lam and throwing him into an exciting chase for freedom and fame.

Reggae had undergone a rapid transformation in Jamaica from calypso to ska and rocksteady before emerging as its very own distinct sound in the 1960s. By the early 1970s, white musicians had caught on to this new sound and were implementing it into their music. Three Dog Night scored a number-one hit with their cover of the reggae song "Black and White" and Paul Simon topped the billboards with his reggae-inspired "Mother and Child Reunion," in which Cliff's backing group sang vocals. Cliff had been a musician since childhood, penning his own music since grade school. He found success in the late '60s managing to score a handful of hit singles. It was his turn as Ivan in *The Harder They Come* that skyrocketed him, Jamaican patois, and reggae into the stratosphere.

The Harder They Come scored as a massive hit in Jamaica, becoming the first film from the country to break out into global cinematic awareness. Henzell, who came from British money and worked overseas as a television commercial producer, brought a fresh take and natural representation of Jamaica that many hadn't seen before. His script with Rhone is filled with brilliant moments of social critique for the corrupt systems and apathetic institutions that all but push Ivan to a life of crime. The filmmakers seem to have empathy for the real-life criminal, presenting Ivan as a man willing to work hard if given the opportunity, but the hypocrisy of local religion, the wealth disparity of the island, and the bureaucracy in place left behind by colonial rule makes this an improbability.

"The oppressors are trying to keep me down, make me feel like I'm a clown. But the

harder they come, the harder they fall. Oh, I know," Ivan sings during his big-break recording session. The lyrics and the rhythmic hook repeat as the film's refrain, reminding audiences of the environment that Ivan is attempting to find success in. During a poignant scene of Ivan watching the Spaghetti Western *Django* (1966) in a lively movie theater, his eyes light up when the hero takes down a group of masked men, a scene that returns during the film's climatic ending. Audiences can't help but root for Ivan; he's the anti-hero on par with those in *Bonnie and Clyde* (1967), *Dillinger* (1945), and *Scarface* (1932).

The Harder They Come went on to become an international success, bringing reggae and the "rude boy" culture of rebellious Jamaican youths to audiences worldwide. Its influence, along with Jimmy Cliff's stardom, helped move Bob Marley into the forefront with his 1974 album *Catch Fire*. Peter Tosh, Johnny Nash, and a number of other reggae stars also gained traction during this time. This burgeoning scene influenced the likes of The Clash, Eric Clapton, The Police, and Boy George, who all incorporated elements of reggae music into their acts while others embraced the rude boy style. *The Harder They Come* is now a cult classic screened across the world and taught to college students as an example of Third Cinema, a film movement birthed in Latin America that aimed at being revolutionary and subverting the standards of Hollywood profiteering and self-indulgent European art.

OPPOSITE: Jimmy Cliff smokes a cigarette on the set.

Genre-ly Speaking

Although *The Harder They Come* is the most recognized film from Jamaica and the West Indies, it's not nearly the only. Other titles from the island and about its peoples in other parts of the world are as follows:

Horace Ové's *Pressure* (1976)

Ted Bafaloukos's *Rockers* (1978)

Franco Rosso's *Babylon* (1980)

Dickie Jobson's *Countryman* (1982)

Isaac Julien's *Young Soul Rebels* (1991)

THE HONEYMOON KILLERS

USA, 1970 • COLOR AND B&W, 107 MINUTES

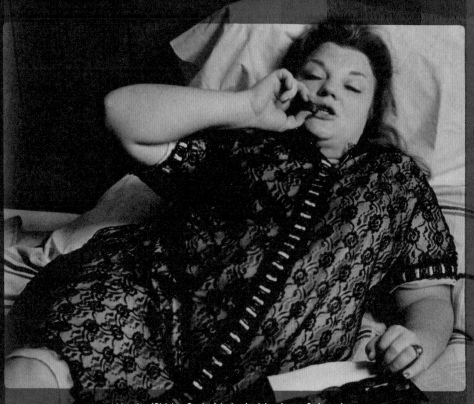

Martha (Shirley Stoler) in bed with a box of chocolates

DIRECTOR: Leonard Kastle **SCREENPLAY:** Leonard Kastle

STARRING: Shirley Stoler (Martha Beck), Tony Lo Bianco (Ray Fernandez), Doris Roberts (Bunny), Mary Jane Higby (Janet Fay), Kip McArdle (Delphine Downing)

One of the most daring independent films released in the period just after the end of the Hollywood Production Code in 1968 is Leonard Kastle's *The Honeymoon Killers*, a fictional retelling of the true crimes of "lonely hearts killers" Martha Beck and Raymond Fernandez in the late 1940s. The film was an answer to the success of Arthur Penn's *Bonnie and Clyde* (1967), a cool, sexy take on the classic crime couple starring Faye Dunaway and Warren Beatty. Kastle, a composer of operas, had never made a movie before, and only directed *The Honeymoon Killers* after two previous directors left the project (one

of them being Martin Scorsese). In fact, the film wasn't even his idea in the first place; he participated at the insistence of his friend and business partner, Warren Steibel, who suggested Kastle write the screenplay. Kastle did his own research on the Beck and Fernandez case and was taken with the idea of making a crime film featuring realistic-looking people; Steibel managed to secure a small budget for the film. The casting of Martha and Ray also seemed a bit serendipitous; both Shirley Stoler and Tony Lo Bianco had come from the theater world and had done little film acting before *The Honeymoon Killers*. Impressively,

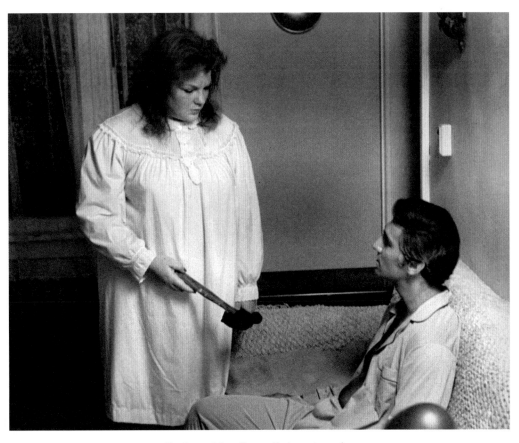

Martha and Ray discuss their next murder.

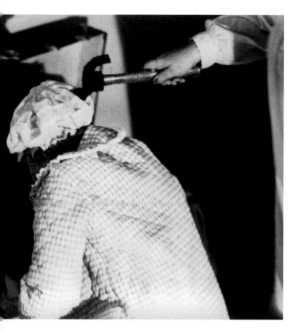

One of the film's most shocking moments as Janet (Mary Jane Higby) meets her unfortunate demise

this group of first-timers managed to churn out a shocking, memorable crime drama that still manages to ruffle feathers to this day.

Martha is a single, overweight nurse living in Florida with her overbearing mother. Her friend Bunny (Doris Roberts) signs her up for a lonely-hearts club that pairs single men and women together as pen pals. She begins an epistolary relationship with a man named Ray, captured in a fantastic montage sequence set to a sweeping number by Gustav Mahler (his music is used throughout the film). After meeting in person, Martha becomes obsessed with Ray, and he confesses he has been using the lonely-hearts service in order to meet middle-aged women and rob them of their money. Instead of balking, Martha decides to join the grift, offering to pose as

his sister as Ray continues to use the service to meet women.

However, jealousy rages in Martha as Ray enacts his game with woman after woman, despite his promises to not have sex with them. Unlike Martha, they share a cheerful naiveté that only unsuspecting victims of a grift have and are essentially the same: white, middle-aged, middle class, and gleefully earnest. One of Ray and Martha's early victims, Doris (Ann Harris) is seen singing "America the Beautiful" in the bathtub while they steal money from her purse in the other room. In the last days of the hippie era (the film was made around the time of the Manson Family murders), these women seem from a much earlier time, an America that seemed to no longer exist.

As the story progresses, it becomes increasingly clear that Martha is not emotionally equipped to be a part of this arrangement. She won't share Ray with anyone, even if their scam depends on it. Soon her jealously spills over into murder; her experience as a nurse makes her an expert at drugging Ray's newest conquest, and the two of them leave her to die on a bus. They're soon on to the next victim as Martha, Ray, and his new girlfriend are at the lake for the day. Martha seethes on the shore while the happy couple are splashing around in the water, then return to their towels to have some alone time. In one of the most memorable scenes in the film, Martha is so overtaken by the situation that she walks into a river and tries to drown herself. Ray has to go in and save her, in a moment that asks several questions: Is Ray still ruthlessly using Martha for his own ends? Did he actually fall in love? How will Martha continue to partici-pate in this game when it obviously hurts her so much?

They then move on to Janet Fay (played by classic radio star Mary Jane Higby), who begins to have her doubts about the brother/sister team. She reluctantly agrees to give Ray a large sum of money, but the couple is still spooked by her suspicions. Martha then enacts one of the most sinister murders in the film as she hits Janet Fay over the head with a claw hammer. The black-and-white cinematography of Oliver Wood (who was originally brought into the project by Scors-ese and stayed after he left) is served par-ticularly well here, making these scenes feel like you're watching news footage instead of a narrative film. The frequent use of ambi-ent lighting and the patchy sound only add to the terror. Eventually their body count includes a child when Ray courts a younger woman and her daughter. The scene of Mar-tha taking the young girl to the basement is positively bone chilling.

This rawness of *The Honeymoon Killers*, which is both visual and emotional, is bold for the moment and deeply unsettling. Shirley Stoler as Martha is easily the best part of the film in this regard, creating a character who is both enraging and sympathetic. Martha is not simply a one-dimensional character, the scorned "ugly fat woman"; Stoler gives her a complexity that compels us to want to understand her humanity, yet be terrified by her actions. Despite taking some liberties with the original crimes, *The Honeymoon Kill-ers* manage to paint an ultra-bleak portrait of a couple driven to extreme measures by greed and desperation. In the tradition of the "lovers on the run" film, it's an especially dark and nihilistic entry, one that tells an unglam-orous, un-Hollywood version of an American crime story.

A Spotlight on . . . Shirley Stoler

Character actress Shirley Stoler (1929–1999) made an impression any time she appeared onscreen. The daughter of Russian immigrants, Stoler worked in experimental theater in New York City in her early career (she often ran in the same circles as cult directors Andy Mil-ligan and Andy Warhol) and made the jump to film with her role as the des-perate Martha in *The Honeymoon Kill-ers*. Often known for playing villains or tough women, she made appearances in *Klute* (1971) and *The Deer Hunter* (1978) and would be praised for her role as the notorious Nazi commandant in Lina Wertmüller's *Seven Beauties* (1975). In addition to her work on Broadway, chil-dren of the 1980s would come to know her as Mrs. Steve, one of the neighbors on *Pee-Wee's Playhouse* (1986–1990), and through her various appearances on both daytime and primetime television. She worked consistently until her death in 1999.

THE SILENT PARTNER

CANADA, 1978 • COLOR, 106 MINUTES

Seasons Greetings from Harry Reikle (Christopher Plummer) as Santa Claus

DIRECTOR: Daryl Duke   **SCREENPLAY:** Curtis Hanson,
based on a novel by Anders Bodelsen
STARRING: Elliott Gould (Miles Cullen), Christopher Plummer (Harry Reikle),
Susannah York (Julie), Céline Lomez (Elaine), John Candy (Simonsen)

Arguably one of the best movies from the Canadian tax-shelter era (see Genre-ly Speaking, page 37) is *The Silent Partner*, a remake of a Danish film called *Think of a Number* (1969), and originally based on a Danish novel of the same name (*Tænk på et tal*) from 1968. Writer/director Curtis Hanson, who was just starting his career, directing his first film for Roger Corman (the 1972 Tab Hunter B-movie thriller *Sweet Kill*), wrote the spec script for *The Silent Partner* in the hope that he would be able to direct it. Instead, the job went to Daryl Duke, a Vancouver native who had started his career as a television producer for the Canadian Broadcasting Corporation before making his debut feature film, *Payday* (1972), starring Rip Torn as a touring country musician.

While a heist movie at its core, *The Silent Partner* has the low and slow simmer of a Hitchcock film. Its main character, Miles Cullen (played by Elliott Gould), becomes entangled in a scheme to rob the bank where he works, located inside a busy shopping mall, during the holidays. Gould was already a movie star by this point, having played one of his most famous roles a few years earlier, that of Raymond Chandler's literary detective Philip Marlowe in Robert Altman's *The Long Goodbye*. Miles has echoes of Philip Marlowe: the suit-and-tie look he wears, the pets he owns (this time it's exotic fish). But whereas Marlowe was lovably rough around the edges, Miles is essentially a stuffy nine-to-five-er suffering from ennui; he's a loner and a bit of a nerd. He seems to be searching for some kind of excitement outside his highly organized, analytical line of work. His father is dying in a

nursing home and he is unable to sort out his true feelings for his work crush, Julie (played by Susannah York). Being involved in a caper is just the kind of exhilaration Miles needs.

Miles finds out very early in the film that a fellow mall employee dressed as Santa Claus for the holidays (Harry Reikle, played by Christopher Plummer) intends to rob the bank after a customer makes his daily big cash deposit. Miles plans to steal the money before Reikle can get to it. The actual robbery gets bungled

Harry Reikle always dressed for the occasion.

FROM LEFT: Elliott Gould as Miles • Elaine (Céline Lomez) and Miles

after Miles sets off the silent alarm, sending the jolly man running from the bank, shooting at the security guard who chases him.

Miles becomes a local celebrity after stopping the heist yet is still holding the money Reikle was intending to steal. Thus begins a crazy cat-and-mouse game between the two, wherein Reikle's evil ruthlessness begins to truly unfold. Reikle is seen wearing fetish clothing, committing a heinous act of cruelty toward a young woman in a bathhouse, suggesting that his character is into sadism, perhaps queer or trans or maybe some combination thereof. Reikle's sexual identity is not addressed in *The Silent Partner* but what is clear is that he is willing to do anything in order to get his money back. He begins to spy on Miles in his own home, calling him on the phone incessantly, even at the bank. Miles comes home one night to find his apartment ransacked and one of his fish stabbed with a knife. Miles decides to fight back, having

Reikle arrested yet failing to identify him in a lineup for fear of being named in the robbery. Reikle still has some more truly evil tricks up his sleeve, however, and the two become even more intertwined—and mutually assured destruction seems downright inevitable. The scenes of public shootouts are especially harrowing, and the complexity of Miles and Reikle's game gives the film a constant anxiety that is hard to ignore.

After his father passes away, at his funeral Miles suddenly meets Elaine (Céline Lomez), a nurse who looked after his father while he was sick. They strike up a relationship and soon it's revealed that she is working as a spy for Reikle while he's been in jail, trying to gain Miles's trust in hopes that he'll tell her where he stashed the money. She ends up actually falling for Miles, however, and it enrages Reikle to the point where he performs another grisly murder, this time using a broken fish tank in Miles's apartment to

Harry Reikle places a menacing phone call.

was notoriously hard for American audiences to track down). And much like *Die Hard*, it has also been celebrated by cult movie fans as an off-beat Christmas classic in recent years.

decapitate her. Miles furthers his involvement with Reikle, however, after he decides to clean up the crime scene at his place and hide Elaine's body. Reikle begins to call Miles "his partner" in both the robbery and the murder, and they make arrangements for Reikle to finally get his money at the bank, with Reikle dressing in drag to go unnoticed. The final shootout with Reikle, which again takes place in the mall, gives the film its memorable and tense conclusion.

The Silent Partner features an early appearance by John Candy, who plays one of Miles's colleagues in the bank. Although he doesn't have many lines, Candy's naturally comedic presence makes him a joy to see whenever he's on-screen. The film was also scored by the great Canadian jazz pianist Oscar Peterson, and it was one of the only film scores he ever did. *The Silent Partner* has been an exciting rediscovery for film fans after finally making its way to Blu-ray in 2019 (before then, it

Genre-ly Speaking

The Capital Cost Allowance was a Canadian government incentive that offered a very generous tax incentive to anyone who invested in films made in their country. The result was a sudden proliferation in film production in the 1970s and 1980s, known informally as the Canadian tax-shelter era. Unsurprisingly, a number of genre films were made with this incentive, as producers found this a cheap, easy way to get a return on their investment. For more horror/thriller gems from the Capital Cost Allowance, check out:

Cannibal Girls (1973)

Black Christmas (1974)

Deranged (1974)

Rabid (1977)

The Brood (1979)

Prom Night (1980)

The Changeling (1980)

My Bloody Valentine (1981)

Scanners (1981)

SHACK OUT ON 101

USA, 1955 • B&W, 80 MINUTES

Slob (Lee Marvin) shoots from the kitchen.

DIRECTOR: Edward Dein **SCREENPLAY:** Edward Dein, Mildred Dein

STARRING: Terry Moore (Kotty), Frank Lovejoy (Prof. Sam Bastion), Keenan Wynn (George), Lee Marvin (Slob), Whit Bissell (Eddie)

One of the strangest and most fascinating films of the 1950s is *Shack Out on 101*, a low-budget noir shot in a very contained environment: a desolate, coastal roadside diner. It concerns a short-order cook/dishwasher at the diner who is discovered moonlighting as a communist spy. By 1955, the Red Scare had certainly infiltrated Hollywood, and movies such as *The Women on Pier 13* (1949) and *My Son John* (1952) had also centered their entire plots on Cold War paranoia. However, *Shack Out on 101* transcends the topical, shock premise to become a tense crime drama with moments of genuine humor and silliness tucked in between. Imagine *The Petrified Forest* by way of *Abbott and Costello* and you might be getting warmer. At many moments, the film feels like a play being acted out by a cadre of amazing character actors whose camaraderie and rhythm have charmed you so much, you'd likely watch them do anything . . . and then actually do. Written by the husband-wife team of Edward and Mildred Dein (and directed by Edward), this quirky tale often veers into unexpected directions and is made all the more entertaining by it.

George is the owner of a small choke and puke located along Highway 101 on the California coast. His employees include Kotty, a pretty, whip-smart blonde waitress whom the guys around the diner call "Tomato" (and are all seemingly in love with), and an uncouth, knuckleheaded short-order cook everyone calls "Slob." The film opens as Kotty is sunbathing on the beach and the lecherous Slob attempts a warped kiss-in-the-sand moment à la Deborah Kerr and Burt Lancaster in *From Here to Eternity*, but Kotty fights him off, thoroughly disgusted. We learn that her main focus is studying for a civil servant's exam so she can quit the restaurant, a patriotic goal she feels will bring her closer to her boyfriend, Sam, a nuclear scientist and professor at the local university. The diner is a meeting place for many of the town locals including Eddie, one of George's sweet but shell-shocked ex-military buddies, and an assortment of poultry truck drivers and fishmongers making deliveries along the 101. All of them seem to have words with Slob at one point or another, and the zippy one-liners always come hard and sharp at him (easily some of the funniest parts of the film). George and Slob's back-and-forth is especially spirited, with Slob seeming to give back as much as he takes. However, in addition to being a sex pest with a mercurial nature, Slob also has a penchant for violence, on full display in the scene where he and a fish delivery guy competitively start wailing on each other in the kitchen, each with an end of a dirty dish towel in their mouths.

Despite their playfulness, Slob and the fishmonger secretly exchange money for a small film container, whereby we discover Slob is actually a foreign spy working against the United States, part of a larger network within the town that is attempting to steal nuclear secrets. George and his staff remain none the wiser until it's eventually revealed that Sam is also in on the arrangement after one of their spy associates is found dead, a conversation that Kotty accidentally walks in on one night. With Kotty now armed with the knowledge that communists have infiltrated the diner, she must decide how to handle the traitorous situation while also trying to sort out her new, complicated love life among all the men in her orbit.

As Slob, actor Lee Marvin, who at this point in his career had played several memorable villains in films such as *The Wild One*, *The Big Heat*, and *Bad Day at Black Rock*, makes a case for his eventual bump up to leading man status in *Shack Out on 101*. His ability to switch between a slimy cook and a member of an international spy organization is both seamless and believable, a true testament to his talent. However, it's great to see Marvin in his goofier moments. In one amusingly odd scene, Slob and George, both shirtless, randomly decide to lift weights inside the restaurant. Marvin and Wynn would become lifelong friends and their closeness is apparent in this scene, as they assess each other's bodies and poke each

accidentally harpoon a giant, stuffed fish hanging on the wall. In an interview with the film noir historian Alan K. Rode and *Shack Out on 101* actress Terry Moore after a 2012 screening of the film, Moore revealed that both of these scenes were totally improvised, and they ultimately would become the most discussed moments of the movie. These comic detours may seem incongruous but instead feel like bursts of fresh air to counter the darker, more claustrophobic moments of the film. For this reason, *Shack Out on 101* ends up a delightful surprise among the crime movies of the era.

Kotty (Terry Moore, center) fends off yet another advance from one of the customers.

OMG Moment

While Shack Out on 101 has many moments of quirky transcendence, one of the best comes near the beginning of the film where Sam and Kotty are engaged in a kiss. During their moment of passion, Kotty insists that Sam quiz her on the Bill of Rights and other governmental matters (so she can pass her civil servant's exam, naturally). The bit goes on for about a beat or two too long, however, and eventually gets to the point where Sam starts whispering in Kotty's ear the merits of the United States of America as a republic. It's enough to make you ask yourself, "Could this be the least sexy pillow talk ever?"

other's stomachs in friendly competition. It's a bizarre pause to take in the middle of this tense story about communism but also, somehow, completely enjoyable. Another strangely light-hearted moment happens between George and Eddie as they try their new skin-diving gear inside the diner. Both actors attempt to walk around in their flippers and masks, then

DOMESTIC DISTURBANCES

"The call is coming from inside the house" has become a well-known and oft-repeated horror tagline over the years because of its simple method of shock: what we fear is much closer than we think. While cult film has largely been defined by the genres of horror, science fiction, and action, TCM Underground has been a longtime champion of tales of strange romances, fractured family relationships, and other twisted stories about the ones we love. Be it the Blands of *Eating Raoul* killing people to fund their family business or Emily stalking through the window of her ex-husband's house in *Remember My Name*, these films may have you looking twice at the people around you—are they really what they seem?

BUTCHER, BAKER, NIGHTMARE MAKER

(A.K.A. NIGHT WARNING)

USA, 1981 • COLOR, 96 MINUTES

You wouldn't want to disappoint your Aunt Cheryl (Susan Tyrrell), would you?

DIRECTOR: William Asher   **SCREENPLAY:** Steve Breimer, Alan Jay Glueckman, Boon Collins

STARRING: Jimmy McNichol (Billy Lynch), Susan Tyrrell (Cheryl Roberts),

Bo Svenson (Detective Joe Carlson), Julia Duffy (Julie Linden), Bill Paxton (Eddie)

One of the most interesting entries among the slasher film craze of the 1980s is William Asher's *Butcher, Baker, Nightmare Maker*, a movie that explores the problematic relationship between a single, over-possessive, and sexually frustrated aunt and her teenage nephew. Asher rose to fame during the Golden Age of television with classic series such as *I Love Lucy*, *The Twilight Zone*, and *Bewitched*, as well as directing and co-writing several of the 1960s Beach Party films starring Annette Funicello and Frankie Avalon. Yet he would move into much darker territory with the film's screenwriters, Stephen Breimer, Boon Collins, and Alan Jay Glueckman, who were inspired by the idea of the female villain in horror movies such as *What Ever Happened to Baby Jane?* (1962) in creating their anti-hero for *Butcher, Baker, Nightmare Maker*, the capricious and memorable Aunt Cheryl.

For this starring role, they tapped the legendary character actress Susan Tyrrell, who had become a hero to cinephiles with her powerful, emotional roles in movies such as *Fat City* (1972), *Andy Warhol's Bad* (1977), and the surrealist cult musical *Forbidden Zone* (1980). Knowing Tyrrell's talent and boldness for taking on intense, complicated women, Asher instructed her to give everything she had to her portrayal as the unhinged Aunt Cheryl, and she did not disappoint. Cast alongside Tyrrell as her nephew, Billy, was the young actor Jimmy McNichol, a child actor turned 1970s teen heartthrob who achieved success alongside his sister, Kristy (in a similar vein to the Osmonds, they also recorded an album together). McNichol's boyish good looks did

not go to waste in the movie, as Billy navigates the strange nature of his aunt's attachment.

After his parents' death in a harrowing car accident left him orphaned as a young child, Billy is looked after by Cheryl, a childless woman who we quickly learn is very possessive of her nephew. She spends her days endlessly doting on him, forcing both a physical and emotional closeness that veers on the uncomfortable. Billy is a star basketball player at his school and wants to accept a full-ride sports scholarship at an out-of-state school that his girlfriend, Julie, is also attending. Aunt Cheryl is horrified by the thought of Billy leaving her alone and guilt-trips him into staying in town, getting a job, and living with her in a room upstairs, which she plans to turn into an apartment for him. Aunt Cheryl begins to drug Billy's milk so that he's unable to play basketball and will just stay in bed so she can nurse him back to health.

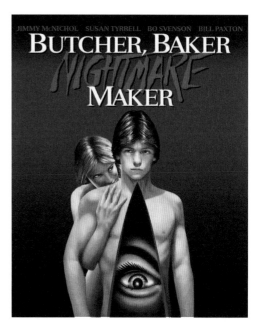

Aunt Cheryl's new self-haircut

Aunt Cheryl, desperate for male attention, makes a sexual advance toward a handyman named Phil Brody (Caskey Swaim). He refuses her, and in retaliation, she stabs him with a giant kitchen knife. Aunt Cheryl claims the handyman attempted to rape her and she was acting in self-defense, gaining sympathy from Billy as the police arrive. An intimidating detective assigned to the case named Joe Carlson (Bo Svenson) immediately suspects Billy had something to do with Brody's murder. Upon finding out Billy's basketball coach, Tom Landers (Steve Eastin), is gay and was in a relationship with Brody, Detective Carlson, who is both a bigot and a homophobe, is convinced Billy is also gay and murdered Brody in a love-triangle-gone-wrong scenario, with very little evidence to support this suspicion.

As Detective Carlson closes in on Billy with his wild theory on the Brody case, his more level-headed colleague Sergeant Cook (Britt Leach) slowly begins to suspect Aunt Cheryl as the real murderer.

It would be easy to pass off *Butcher, Baker, Nightmare Maker* as standard early 1980s slasher fare, and there is enough carnage to satisfy the most discerning horror movie fan. However, certain elements of the film stand out beyond this, especially the larger-than-life performances of both Tyrrell and Svenson. The movie's ties to melodrama and Grande Dame Guignol are apparent; much like the Bette Davis character from *What Ever Happened to Baby Jane?*, Aunt Cheryl's desperation for love and understanding is the reason she traps a family member into staying with her forever. Despite the character conventions, however, the moment her frustration turns homicidal is both unexpected and chilling. Another unique aspect of the film is

Aunt Cheryl checks on Billy (Jimmy McNichol) in the shower.

the way Coach Landers's sexuality is treated. As a gay character in an early '80s movie, he isn't the comic relief or the villain; instead, his sexuality is seen as a simple matter of fact. His relationship with Brody before his death was normal and faithful by all accounts, and when he's outed by Detective Carlson, it's Billy who insists on protecting him from both the puritanical judgments of Aunt Cheryl (who calls him "sick") and the rampant, unrelenting homophobia of Carlson. Additionally, the character of Billy toward the end of the film is a fresh turn in the concept of the "final girl," as are the people who inevitably come to his aid. *Butcher, Baker, Nightmare Maker* offers a slew of confounding twists on the typical slasher genre and stands as a salacious cinematic oddity today.

A Spotlight on . . . Susan Tyrrell

Charismatic, playful, and highly emotional, the character actress Susan Tyrrell left a lasting impression on film before her death in 2012. If you're looking for more of her iconic appearances, seek out the following:

Fat City (1972)

Andy Warhol's Bad (1976)

I Never Promised You a Rose Garden (1977)

Forbidden Zone (1980)

Cry-Baby (1990)

EATING RAOUL

USA, 1982 • COLOR, 90 MINUTES

The Blands (Paul Bartel and Mary Woronov) have a payday.

DIRECTOR: Paul Bartel   **SCREENPLAY:** Paul Bartel, Richard Blackburn

STARRING: Mary Woronov (Mary Bland), Paul Bartel (Paul Bland), Robert Beltran

(Raoul Mendoza), Susan Saiger (Doris the Dominatrix), Buck Henry (Mr. Leech)

The legendary B-movie producer Roger Corman is responsible for launching the careers of several of Hollywood's most-loved creatives, including the collaboration between the cult film actress Mary Woronov and the cult director/actor Paul Bartel. Woronov made her film debut in 1966 as part of Andy Warhol's inner circle when she appeared in Warhol's *Chelsea Girls*. In that same year, Bartel released his first independent short film, *The Secret Cinema*. They ran in similar crowds in these early years, but it wasn't until they both worked for Corman on the Bartel-directed 1975 science fiction/action satire *Death Race 2000* that the two would become lifelong coconspirators and friends, often-times playing husband and wife (despite not being romantically involved in real life). They were paired in seventeen different projects over three decades, but their best and most famous film remains *Eating Raoul*, a subversive nod to the crime comedies of Britain's Ealing Studios and the husband-wife teams of the classic screwball era. The dark comedy effectively cemented Woronov and Bartel as the Doris Day and Rock Hudson of B movies.

Here, the two play Mary and Paul Bland, a childless married couple living in Los Angeles. Paul, a fine wine enthusiast, works at a low-rent liquor store and is fired one day after placing an order for an extremely expensive product the owner refuses to sell. Mary is a registered dietician at a local hospital where she is constantly harassed and groped by every man she meets. The apartment building where the Blands live is filled with neighbors who host regular swingers parties, much to their dismay. Instead, the Blands sleep in twin beds, wear matching formal pajamas to bed, and are seemingly never intimate. Desperate to escape to the suburbs where they can realize their dream of owning a restaurant yet unable to come up with the money, inspiration hits one night by way of a local dominatrix, who tells them just how easy it is to make fast money from men looking to satisfy specific sexual fetishes. Figuring they could not only earn the cash for their eatery but also rid their community of the sexual deviancy they find disgusting, the couple takes out an ad in the local alternative newspaper, luring potential johns to their apartment. The Blands formulate an outrageous murderous scheme involving a cast-iron frying pan that brings them closer to their "country kitchen" dream.

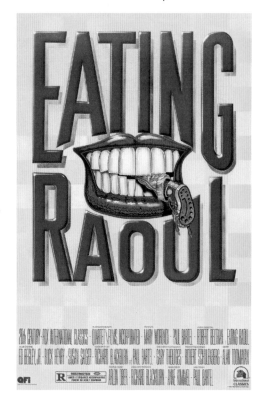

Paul and Mary Bland in the happiest place on earth

When asked about the inspiration for *Eating Raoul*, Bartel frequently mentioned the Ealing masterpieces *Kind Hearts and Coronets* (1949) and *The Ladykillers* (1955), starring the legendary comic actor Sir Alec Guinness. Both films are classic black comedies in which murder is part of the humor. In this regard, *Raoul* feels connected to this tradition, albeit with a few more salacious details thrown in the mix. The Blands, for all their transgressive hijinks, have a rapport about them reminiscent of a modern version of Nick and Nora Charles from *The Thin Man* or even characters from a classic Katharine Hepburn–Cary Grant comedy. Alongside the more effervescent moments, however, *Eating Raoul* is also rife with social commentary, especially about white middle-class fears of the big city, specifically Los Angeles, where Paul Bland's bigoted comments toward Mexicans seem to come as quickly as his distaste for the "rich perverts" of Hollywood. The Blands' fervent obsession with the sex lives of others is a major element in the film and is especially ironic considering how passionless their own marriage seems to be.

Mary Bland in policewoman fetish gear

In a feature full of unexpected delights, the greatest joy of *Eating Raoul* is seeing Bartel and Woronov acting together. As with any famous creative pairing, their screen time together always feels fun and friendly, making us wish we could join their secret club, no matter how absurd their predicament. *Raoul* also boasts a parade of great character actors as L.A.'s finest freaks, including Ed Begley Jr., Groundlings performers John Paragon and Edie McClurg, and Buck Henry in an especially outrageous role.

A Spotlight on . . . Paul Bartel and Mary Woronov

Endlessly entertaining cult movie coconspirators Paul Bartel and Mary Woronov appeared together many times over the course of their careers. Here are some of our favorites:

Death Race 2000 (1975)

Hollywood Boulevard (1976)

Rock 'n' Roll High School (1979)

Chopping Mall [reprising their roles as the Blands] (1986)

Scenes from the Class Struggle in Beverly Hills (1989)

POLYESTER

USA, 1981 • COLOR, 86 MINUTES

Francine (Divine) gets a surprise in her kitchen.

DIRECTOR: John Waters   **SCREENPLAY:** John Waters
STARRING: Divine (Francine Fishpaw), Tab Hunter (Todd Tomorrow),
Edith Massey (Cuddles Kovinsky), Mary Garlington (Lu-Lu Fishpaw),
Ken King (Dexter Fishpaw)

Writer-director John Waters spent most of the 1960s and 1970s making his signature outrageous independent films with his Baltimore-based coconspirators, the Dreamlanders. However, it wasn't until the early 1980s that Waters got his first shot at a bona fide studio picture when Robert Shaye's New Line Productions branched out from film distribution into creating original pictures. New Line had distributed Waters's earlier films *Multiple Maniacs*, *Female Trouble*, and *Desperate Living*, and his new film, *Polyester*, would be one of their earliest in-house productions, benefiting from a budget much larger than Waters had been accustomed to. Thus, *Polyester* became the first R-rated John Waters film, meaning it had a wider theatrical release than his prior films, which were either X or unrated (and typically screened at colleges and at smaller, art-house cinemas). However, this fact should not signal to anyone that *Polyester* isn't as transgressive as Waters's most notorious tales of shock. Instead, the film uses satire to comment on puritanical American values via the style of the picturesque 1950s melodramas made famous by director Douglas Sirk. *Polyester* is essentially a women's picture with a giant foot stomp, a housewife fantasy film in which a drag queen plays the role usually inhabited by a classic screen siren such as Elizabeth Taylor and is eventually courted by a guy who *actually was* a classic screen hunk, actor Tab Hunter. And in another nod to a filmmaker of the era, B-movie pioneer William Castle, Waters created a movie gimmick within the world of *Polyester* called Odorama, which employed the use of scratch-and-sniff cards

handed out to moviegoers, prompting them to breathe in the scent of the corresponding number as it flashed on the screen.

Waters's muse and cult movie icon Divine (born Harris Glenn Milstead) reveled in the leading role of Francine Fishpaw, a Baltimore housewife trying to keep her family together. Francine's husband, Elmer (played by David Samson), runs a local porno theater that is being protested by the religious right, which he loves because it garners more publicity for his business. He spends his days berating and ordering around his wife and showing affection only toward the family dog, Bonkers. Perhaps a nod to the bratty children that attempt to sabotage Jane Wyman's happiness in *All That Heaven Allows* (the family hilariously lives at 538 Wyman

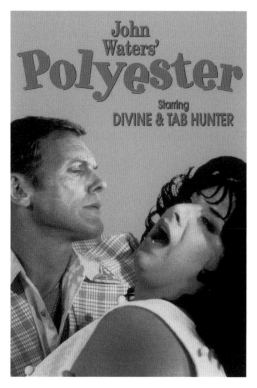

Way), Francine's children are terrible to an exaggerated degree. Her daughter, Lu-Lu (Garlington), is the consummate party girl, constantly seen go-go dancing (even while she's talking) and so singularly interested in only having a good time she can't open a bottle of soda without spraying it everywhere like a sports team winning the Super Bowl. Her son, Dexter (King), frequently sniffs glue and creepily gets off on pictures of women's shoes, moonlighting as the Baltimore Foot Stomper, a notorious local criminal who waits for women outside stores and stomps on their feet with orgasmic glee. Francine's own mother, La Rue (played by Joni Ruth White), even holds her in high contempt, gleefully criticizing her daughter at every turn while stealing money from her wallet.

Francine's only real friend is Cuddles Kovinsky (played by Dreamlander favorite Edith Massey). Formerly her housekeeper, she now relishes the life of the nouveau riche after getting a hefty inheritance from one of her clients. Cuddles offers to take Francine shopping to alleviate the constant barrage of misery, which Francine is so conditioned to tolerate that she still manages to make nice meals for her family and say her prayers every night. Francine also possesses an extraordinary sense of smell (remember the Odorama cards?) that alerts her to the fact that her husband is cheating with his secretary, Sandra Sullivan (played by another Waters regular, Mink Stole, sporting one of her most memorable on-screen hairstyles). Even when Francine and Cuddles catch them together

Divine as Francine Fishpaw

Dr. Arnold Quackenshaw (Rick Breitenfeld) explains the technology behind Odorama.

in a trashy motel, Elmer just laughs and fat-shames her, daring her to divorce him.

Francine's cartoonishly bad home life is a send-up of many classic women's picture tropes, which frequently piled the drama on to otherwise sweet, unassuming mothers and wives. In *Polyester*, most of Francine's shocking reveals are even scored with hilarious organ music cues, a technique often used in old television soap operas. In another borrowed story line from the Golden Age melodrama (see 1947's *Smash-Up: The Story of a Woman*), Francine soon turns to alcoholism, spiraling out of control in her own house as her husband and his mistress prank call her and have pizzas sent to her door. Simultaneously, both Lu-Lu and Dexter's lifestyles finally catch up with them. Lu-Lu becomes pregnant by her scuzzy boyfriend Bo-Bo (played by real-life punk rocker Stiv Bators) and provocatively tells her mother she "can't wait" to have an abortion while Dexter is arrested for his foot-stomping crimes and sent to jail. Tucked into these scenes are plenty of hysterical Waters-trademarked send-ups of the Catholic Church, nosy neighbors, and other American institutions.

As Francine seemingly reaches rock bottom, she begins to notice a handsome man named Todd Tomorrow (Hunter) staring at her during trips into town. At the same time, Dexter eventually returns from prison, now sober and an artist. Lu-Lu's also returned fresh from an unwed mothers' home complacent and reformed by the art of macramé. It all convinces Francine to get sober, which allows her

to finally engage with the mysterious dream man. Tab Hunter was nearly fifty years old when he made *Polyester* and still very much the dreamboat as he was in his 1950s heyday. Like many stars from the classic Hollywood era, Hunter's career had stalled slightly after the end of the studio system but was revived in the 1980s, largely due to his appearance in *Polyester*. Even in his tacky slacks and sport coat, his smile and natural handsomeness make him the perfect Douglas Sirk leading man, the Ron Kirby for Francine's Cary Scott, and she jumps at the opportunity to go for a ride in his Corvette. Their scenes together, which include joyfully skipping through a field (to a ballad called "The Best Thing," sung by comedic actor Bill Murray), are actually kind of beautiful for being a parody of the corny romance montages seen in many women's pictures. Todd's sweet southern drawl and politeness are intoxicating to the underappreciated Francine. He manages to say all the things she wants to hear, including complimenting her French provincial home decor and her innate beauty and sex appeal. He even owns a classy drive-in movie theater that plays Marguerite Duras films instead of the lurid pornos that her husband's business screens. Naturally, Francine's happiness cannot last, as it's revealed Todd was actually hired by her mother (who, as it turns out, is also Todd's lover) to steal her money and send her to a mental institution. It's only with the

OPPOSITE FROM TOP: LuLu Fishpaw (Mary Garlington) does a dance for her boyfriend Bo-Bo (Stiv Bators) and friend. • Francine Fishpaw with Todd Tomorrow (Tab Hunter)

help of her friend Cuddles and her reformed children that Francine finally finds peace by the end of the film.

Many of the other actors in John Waters's regular stable, including Mary Vivian Pierce, Cookie Mueller, and Jean Hill, also manage to sneak into small roles throughout *Polyester*. But the real star is Divine, who powers through every disappointment Francine experiences as expertly as any Sirkian heroine would. Through each sniff and over-the-top plot twist, *Polyester* is a euphoric homage to the melodrama that is very much in the spirit of vintage John Waters, despite being his first mainstream film.

A Spotlight on . . . Tab Hunter and Divine

Polyester would not be the last time Divine (1945–1988) and Tab Hunter (1931–2018) worked together. A few years later, they appeared together in Paul Bartel's comedy *Lust in the Dust* (1985), a send-up of the 1946 Gregory Peck–fronted western *Duel in the Sun*. Hunter believed in the project so much that he produced the film himself and eventually met his life partner, Allan Glaser, while pitching the film to Fox. Glaser subsequently left his job at the studio for *Lust in the Dust* and the new couple raised the money themselves to make the film. The Western parody holds the distinction of being the first movie Divine appeared in that wasn't directed by John Waters.

POSSESSION

FRANCE/WEST GERMANY, 1981 • COLOR, 124 MINUTES

Heinrich (Heinz Bennent) has a confrontation with Anna (Isabelle Adjani).

DIRECTOR: Andrzej Zulawski **SCREENPLAY:** Andrzej Zulawski, Frederic Tuten
STARRING: Isabelle Adjani (Anna), Sam Neill (Mark), Margit Carstensen (Margit Gluckmeister), Heinz Bennent (Heinrich), Johanna Hofer (Heinrich's Mother)

Polish director Andrzej Zulawski was embroiled in crisis in the 1970s. After a very tense, rocky divorce with his wife, the actress Malgorzata Braunek, in 1976, and the censorship and complete shutdown of his science fiction film *On the Silver Globe* by the then-communist Polish government in 1977, Zulawski channeled all his emotions into *Possession*, a film shot in West Berlin during the Cold War. Concerning a couple on the brink of a breakup and their (sometimes depraved) desires to find better versions of their partners, *Possession* is set among the backdrop of the Berlin Wall and the fraught, fractured state of Germany in this era. Written with the American writer Frederic Tuten, Zulawski's screenplay was an incendiary mix of terrifying visuals and histrionic emotions, mirroring the pain and disappointment of Zulawski's personal life. At times it's unclear if the film fits neatly into one genre or across several: a body horror film meets an erotic thriller, a psychological drama mixed with a political polemic. The fact that it was heavily edited when it was eventually released in the United States, and only later achieved its cult status thanks to home video, is a testament to the film's bizarre nature and gut-wrenching intensity.

For the lead role of Anna, Zulawski and producer Marie-Laure Reyre approached the French film star Isabelle Adjani, who had already given several memorable performances, including the lead in Francois Truffaut's *The Story of Adèle H.*, for which she received an Academy Award nomination for Best Actress (at twenty years old, she was the youngest to be nominated at the time). Zulawski and Reyre were also impressed with Aussie director Gillian Armstrong's period drama *My Brilliant Career* after seeing it on the festival circuit, and both wanted

Mark (Sam Neill) confronts Heinrich.

ABOVE: Anna and Mark (Sam Neill) during the film's final moments LEFT: Leslie Malton and Sam Neill

its lead actor, New Zealander Sam Neill, for the role of Mark. A crucial component would be a designer and creator for the infamous tentacled creature of *Possession*. The filmmakers first approached the famous Swiss artist H. R. Giger, fresh off his special-effect work in Ridley Scott's *Alien* (1979), but he was too busy to do the film. Instead, Giger suggested his *Alien* colleague, the Italian FX artist Carlo Rambaldi, to work with Zulawski on his specific vision for the monster at the center of the film.

Possession begins as Anna and Mark, a married couple living in West Berlin, have recently separated. It's clear that Anna is the one who has asked for the divorce, primarily because

Mark's job as a spy keeps him away from the family for long stretches of time. The decision to divorce has upended Mark's emotional state, leaving him anguished and fragile; the couple violently screams at each other in their home and in public, typically taking out their frustrations on any inanimate object that stands in the way. Mark is soon horrified to realize their son has been left alone in the apartment for long stretches of time while Anna goes out, and he makes the immediate decision to take custody of his son. Yet, when Mark is walking him to school one morning, he suddenly realizes his son's teacher looks exactly like Anna. The teacher has green eyes instead of brown, and unlike Anna, she exudes a pleasant, soft, doting temperament that Mark finds warm and comforting; he decides he wants to spend more time with her.

Soon Mark decides to hire a private investigator (Carl Duering) to track Anna's whereabouts. The investigator soon discovers she's been renting a squalid apartment in Kreuzberg and decides to enter the building. To his horror, he finds Anna hiding a strange, monster-like creature in the back bedroom. Anna's protection over this creature finally culminates in Mark's discovery of the beast, after showing up to her apartment himself, and seeing the monster and Anna having intercourse. In the violent ending to the film, both Mark and Anna have a reckoning with the status of their relationship, and also the doppelganger of Anna that Mark has found and, of course, the monster at the center of Anna's obsession.

Both Isabelle Adjani and Sam Neill have, at separate moments, called *Possession* one of the most difficult projects they've ever worked on. As evidence, one only has to look to Anna's scene in the subway station, thrashing along the floor and walls as she smashes a gallon of milk for several minutes, finally ending with Anna in a pool of her own fluids and viscera as she has a miscarriage. It is without a doubt the most intense moment of the film and likely the best-known scene. (It's been referenced several times in recent years, including the music video for the song "Voodoo in my Blood" by Massive Attack featuring the Young Fathers, in which the actress Rosamund Pike plays the role of Anna.) Adjani's commitment to the role in that moment is simply stunning, truly giving the film its title. An unmistakably personal work from a director attempting to make art in a creatively restrictive political environment, *Possession* is possibly cult cinema at its most emotional and urgent.

OMG Moment

While it can be argued that *Possession*, as a film, is one, giant OMG Moment, an especially standout scene in the film is the discovery of Anna having sex with the monster. Deeply unsettling and grotesque, it's made worse with Anna's repeating of the word "almost" to a stunned Mark, who views the scene from the bedroom doorway after finally discovering where his wife has been. The whole thing is likely to give you nightmares or at least a very long pause in bewildered thought.

REMEMBER MY NAME

USA, 1978 • COLOR, 94 MINUTES

Geraldine Chaplin stars as the emotional and unpredictable Emily.

DIRECTOR: Alan Rudolph **SCREENPLAY:** Alan Rudolph
STARRING: Geraldine Chaplin (Emily), Anthony Perkins (Neil Curry), Moses
Gunn (Pike), Berry Berenson (Barbara Curry), Jeff Goldblum (Mr. Nudd)

A protégé of the legendary director Robert Altman, filmmaker Alan Rudolph's slow-burn melodrama *Remember My Name* often feels as atmospheric and mysterious as Altman's psychological thriller *3 Women*. Rudolph's take on the classic era of the "women's picture," whose tales of female repression and disappointment were rendered elegant by the likes of Douglas Sirk and Max Ophüls in the 1940s and '50s, *Remember My Name* carries with it a much darker tale of female revenge, as recent parolee Emily begins to stalk her ex-husband, Neil, and his new wife, Barbara (played by the real-life couple Anthony Perkins and Berry Berenson), in an effort to win back his love.

As Emily, Geraldine Chaplin, daughter of the pioneering silent movie star Charlie Chaplin, was no stranger to either Altman or Rudolph, appearing in multiple films by both directors over the course of her career. Her starring turn in *Remember My Name* was a sandbox for her to explore a character who is at once wounded and antagonistic. And much like Sissy Spacek's character of Millie in the Altman drama, our fascination with Emily also rests in the discomfort of never really knowing her or her motivations. The result is a moody 1970s thriller anchored by the hypnotic Chaplin, in one of the best performances of her career.

The words of legendary blues singer Alberta Hunter singing, "I dreamed the man I love has another lover in my place," sets the tone for the beginning of *Remember My Name*, as Emily drives toward the construction site where her ex-husband Neil works. She's just served a twelve-year prison sentence for killing a woman Neil had an affair with, and they haven't seen each other since. Emily silently watches Neil from the car before driving away to a shopping mall, where she purchases a brand-new dress and gets her hair done. After a dehumanizing jail sentence, she begins to carve out a new life, renting a shabby apartment and taking a job as a cashier at a discount store managed by Mr. Nudd, whose own mother was in jail alongside Emily and who has been steadily giving work to ex-cons. We watch as Emily's first shift is overseen by Rita (played by the actress Alfre Woodard, in her very first film) and quickly realize how antisocial and out of practice with the world Emily has become when she starts smoking cigarettes at the register after being told she shouldn't. Chaplin's acting in these scenes is especially standout, her body language and stride matching the uneasy feeling of being back in public.

Just as she is attempting to reenter society, Emily is also raising the stakes with both Neil and Barbara. She begins frequently showing up to their house, uprooting flowers, breaking windows, and watching them intently. Eventually Emily is bold enough to enter the Curry residence as Barbara is home alone, making dinner. Barbara just happens to be holding a giant knife in her hands when Emily, who has been sneaking up from behind, appears, then terrifyingly pulls her own knife out on Barbara before quickly leaving. Chaplin's eyes flash menacingly and look unhinged during the encounter, a testament to her talent at communicating complex emotions through her face, and it becomes a truly scary moment of the film. After Emily is arrested for the

ABOVE: Robert Altman mentoring the director Alan Rudolph
OPPOSITE: Neil (Anthony Perkins) and Emily reunite.

home invasion, Neil is finally forced to stand face-to-face with his ex-wife, and both realize their intense connection comes from a mutual obsession that was possibly never extinguished.

Much like the ambiguity and dream-like pacing of *3 Women*, *Remember My Name* never readily gives you the answers you're looking for. The film's relative obscurity since its release (it has never appeared on home video), especially given the breadth of talent associated with the movie, is also a puzzle to be solved. While those seeking a tidy narrative structure might be left cold by the film, for others, there is a real pleasure in slowly drinking in the tiny details. The news reports on the television, the close-ups of Emily's eyes in the rearview mirror as she's driving,

and the long looks from various characters as they've been subjected to the wrath of Emily provide clues to these characters' identities. Sound is also equally important in the film, with two recurring motifs: the sound of her jail cell that plays any time Emily is lying in her bed and the sound of airplanes flying over the Curry house triggers thoughts of emotional prisons and escapes. However, perhaps one of the very best tells is in the third act of the film, during the reunion scene between Neil and Emily. To get to know each other again, they attempt to order every drink on the bar menu. Neil tells the bartender, "Two Zombies," and in that tiny moment, you wonder if *Remember My Name* is a movie that's simply about reviving the dead.

Did You Know

The legendary film and stage actor Anthony Perkins was cast in *Remember My Name* after Alan Rudolph's wife saw Perkins in a Broadway production of *Equus*. Initially critics didn't buy Perkins as a construction worker in the film, and that opinion was not lost on the actor himself, who felt wholly unqualified to play Neil when filming began and almost walked off the film entirely. It was Rudolph that eventually convinced him to stay.

SECRET CEREMONY

UK, 1968 • COLOR, 109 MINUTES

Elizabeth Taylor as Leonora

DIRECTOR: Joseph Losey   **SCREENPLAY:** George Tabori

STARRING: Elizabeth Taylor (Leonora), Mia Farrow (Cenci), Robert Mitchum (Albert), Peggy Ashcroft (Hannah), Pamela Brown (Hilda)

The American director Joseph Losey made only five feature-length films in his home country before he was exiled to England in 1953 after being named before the House Un-American Activities Committee. Before his Hollywood blacklisting, he primarily made studio pictures, most notably the children's fantasy *The Boy with Green Hair* and a remake of Fritz Lang's 1931 classic *M*. After arriving in Europe, however, Losey began making the films he would be best known for, with a style wholly unique in both artistry and storytelling. Three of his best-remembered films were all made in Europe and were collaborations with playwright Harold Pinter (*The Servant*, *Accident*, and *The Go-Between*). But it was Losey's partnership with arguably the most famous couple in the world in the 1960s, Elizabeth Taylor and Richard Burton, that produced the most ambitious, notorious, and visually stunning films of his career: the Tennessee Williams adaptation *Boom!* and the Gothic psychological thriller *Secret Ceremony*.

Released in the same year, both were deemed disasters by critical and box-office standards, with appraisals at the time placing them firmly in the category of gaudy, bloated art films. Both were financed almost entirely because of the Burtons' participation and featured stories of women who used their homes as protection, with the house itself becoming a manifestation of their traumas. Stylistically, however, they couldn't have been more different. *Boom!* saw the Hollywood couple at odds inside an all-white, ultra-modern, seaside lair as Burton's Christopher Flanders attempts to woo the terminally ill Sissy Goforth (played by Taylor). *Secret Ceremony*,

on the other hand, saw Taylor acting without Burton, dressed in black and hiding out in a gorgeously baroque mansion in moody London. The director noted his use of memorable homes by remarking, "I think places are actors." In *Secret Ceremony*, the house that brings the two main characters together is the true star of the show, filled with antique furniture, stained glass, Tiffany lamps, and ornate fixtures. Losey's longtime art director Richard Macdonald, who was elemental in creating the contrasting atmospheres for both *Boom!* and *Secret Ceremony*, scouted the actual house Leonora and Cenci would use as their hideaway.

Judged for being too much style, not enough substance, there is actually a very dark tale nestled inside the Gothic interiors of *Secret Ceremony*. Taylor's Leonora is a sex worker still reeling over the death of her young daughter in a drowning accident. As she is riding the bus one afternoon, she's approached by a young woman named Cenci, who has been living alone in a London mansion after losing her mother. Cenci was left a fortune after her death, and it's revealed she bears a striking resemblance to Leonora. The two end up going home together and Leonora starts noticing that Cenci acts much, much younger than her actual age (she's roughly about twenty years old), a fact that at times disturbs her. As the days pass, the two women begin to be surrogates for each other's lost relatives. Cenci's middle-aged aunts Hannah and Hilda (played by Peggy Ashcroft and Pamela Brown) arrive at the house regularly to pillage expensive items for their antique store and Cenci's former stepfather, Alfred

Leonora bathes with Cenci (Mia Farrow).

(played by Robert Mitchum), also begins showing up again. Alfred's sexual and mental abuse of Cenci has been long-standing and twisted, and Cenci's response has been to act out their encounters alone in the kitchen, all while a horrified Leonora looks on from another room.

The nasty way Alfred reacts to Leonora is a particularly cringeworthy point in the film, as are other moments, especially when the mother-daughter relationship between Leonora and Cenci veers in questionable directions. Certainly the scene where they bathe together in the giant master bathtub comes to mind, and another when Cenci offers to give Leonora a massage and then begins licking her back. For all the unsettling moments of *Secret Ceremony*, the film

Cenci gives Leonora a backrub.

is inevitably about tragedy, the ways in which two incredibly complex women go about replacing something they've each lost, and the house that brings them together.

Secret Ceremony was among several films Elizabeth Taylor made in the 1960s and 1970s that are in sharp contrast to her early days as a gorgeous Hollywood ingénue. These later period films, which are mostly genre pictures ranging from psychological thrillers to slightly unhinged melodramas, are fascinating for Taylor's fearlessness when it came to appearing vulgar. In *Secret Ceremony*, Taylor really lets the curse words fly and, in one scene, is seen stuffing her face full of food and then burping loudly. Before Taylor assumed the role of Leonora, it was originally offered to Ingrid Bergman (who turned it down). Meanwhile, there were dozens of actresses who tested for the role of Cenci, with Mia Farrow eventually winning the part. Interestingly enough, Losey cast her due to her performance in the TV series *Peyton Place*, not *Rosemary's Baby*, which he actually hadn't seen (it had not been released to the public yet). A bizarre tale of codependence featuring a Hollywood legend and an up-and-coming young star, all nestled inside an emotionally haunted Gothic mansion, *Secret Ceremony* is one of Losey's most misunderstood but fascinating masterpieces.

A Spotlight On . . .
Joseph Losey

Prolific, political, and poetic, the director Joseph Losey began his career stateside but his full blossom would only occur after he was exiled to England during the Hollywood Blacklist. To sample some of his filmography, seek out the following:

Eva (1962)

The Servant (1963)

These Are the Damned (1963)

Accident (1967)

Boom! (1968)

The Go-Between (1971)

Director Joseph Losey on set with Mia Farrow and Elizabeth Taylor

SOMETIMES AUNT MARTHA DOES DREADFUL THINGS

USA, 1971 • COLOR, 95 MINUTES

Aunt Martha (Abe Zwick) gets dressed.

DIRECTOR: Thomas Casey   **SCREENPLAY:** Thomas Casey
STARRING: Abe Zwick (Paul), Wayne Crawford (Stanley), Don Craig (Hubert), Robin Hughes (Vicki), Yanka Mann (Mrs. Adams)

The state of Florida has contributed much to the exploitation genre over the decades, from some of cult movies' most celebrated directors such as Doris Wishman, Bob Clark, David F. Friedman, and Herschell Gordon Lewis. A surprisingly effective entry is one-and-done director Thomas Casey's crime thriller *Sometimes Aunt Martha Does Dreadful Things*. As one of many films that appeared in the wake of Alfred Hitchcock's *Psycho*, it borrows some of the horror and noir aspects from the original, adding several instances of high camp and melodrama, packaging it all in the low-budget cinema tradition the state would later be infamous for. Additionally, the film's centering of a gay couple just a few years after the Stonewall riots and the end of the Production Code would be part of a brief spike in LGBTQ-themed movies, both in Hollywood and in the genre circuit. Yet it's uncertain if the filmmakers were even aware of the sociopolitical implications inherent in their movie, or that they even knew they were choosing to discuss a very textured and complicated gay relationship within their story. *Sometimes Aunt Martha* ends up being delightfully more interesting and well made than it has any right to be: a film that doesn't seem to be trying too hard to be weird, despite featuring a handful of coconspirators from the Sunshine State's somewhat mysterious exploitation movie scene and plenty of bizarre moments indicative of the region's B-movie filmmaking tradition.

A middle-aged woman named Martha Baxter is seen running errands, eventually returning to her house, nested in a quiet neighborhood in South Florida. The neighbors across the street, the pregnant Mrs. Adams (Mann) and her younger daughter Vicki (Hughes), have been curious about their neighbor and try to stop her for a chat. However, Martha is clearly annoyed and evades further conversation by the ringing telephone inside. When Martha answers the phone, we discover that she is actually Paul, played by Abe Zwick (although it's basically clear Martha is a man in drag) and on the line is Stanley (Wayne Crawford), a younger man who has allegedly been out all day, much to Paul's dismay.

The first five minutes of the film reveal the dynamic between the two main characters.

A twisted mind snaps... and a wave of terror begins.

SOMETIMES AUNT MARTHA DOES DREADFUL THINGS

R RESTRICTED — IN COLOR — Starring Scott Lawrence Abe Zwick — A PALMETTO PICTURES RELEASE

From a modern lens, Paul and Stanley would be seen as a gay couple. And even in 1971, it is implied there is *some* kind of romantic relationship between them but never directly addressed in the film. Even as Paul quickly drops the facade of Martha, he still nags Stanley to come home and stop messing around (Stanley is currently at the beach with a woman). After hanging up, Paul immediately goes to the refrigerator, pops open a beer, and begins throwing darts at a poster of a woman, all while cursing Stanley's name and saying aloud to himself, "You're not gonna torment me, baby!" and refusing the "royal shafting" he perceives Stanley is giving him. Clearly this relationship has a lot of baggage, the extent of which the audience is only beginning to understand.

The secret that Paul has previously committed a murder is shown in a brief flashback using a negative image effect, jarring music, and rapid editing. As he begins to remove his Martha outfit in the bedroom, he chooses to leave the skirt, pantyhose, and heels on, as he paces around the room nervously. Paul stares at an old photo of him and Stanley, arm in arm in bathing suits, perhaps during happier days. Whether Stanley is gay, bisexual, or straight is unclear; all we know is his current cavorting seems to be at the center of Paul's frustration. Stanley eventually does come home, arm in arm with Alma (played by Marty Cordova), the girl from the beach and someone he knows from the local pizza joint (which is aptly named Pizza Place). Paul warns Stanley that his "Aunt Martha doesn't enjoy" him "going out with girls." Alma manages to get him into the bedroom, however, and gets

completely naked before Stanley suddenly freaks out and screams for Paul's help. Paul is ready and willing to chase the young woman out of the house, track her into the woods next to the home, and bludgeon her with a knife. It's clear from this scene that Stanley is actually afraid of having sex with women, yet the reason why is never explained in the film, adding another fascinating layer to the relationship between him and Paul.

The next day, the two are in the kitchen and Paul is quick to remind him just how lucky he is to have him around. Paul claims to "not enjoy" the fact that he "has to dress as a woman," implying that Stanley is actually the one that committed the murder, under the influence of drugs, and that's why both men are on the run. (Stanley thoroughly denies it.) Even as Paul claims his female impersonating is merely a disguise, in this scene he can't avoid coming across as camp, wearing a woman's bright blue housecoat, mixing pancake batter, and bitching about Stanley's bad behavior as if he was a mother needling her ungrateful hippie son *while also* being a put-upon housewife who has had it with her no-good husband. While this is happening, Stanley is antagonizing Paul with his own Aunt Martha wig, which, appropriately enough, bears a vague resemblance to Elizabeth Taylor's hairdo in *Who's Afraid of Virginia Woolf*.

Paul's frustration grows as Stanley continues to be fascinated with women. At the same time, Stanley runs into an old Baltimore cohort, Hubert (Don Craig). The man admits he has nowhere to stay and Stanley takes him home to an (again) agitated

Aunt Martha in her living room

Paul-dressed-as-Martha, where he quickly discovers their new houseguest is a heroin addict. With Paul's paranoia on high, he is convinced Hubert knows about the murder in Baltimore, and therefore he must kill him. But Hubert has plans of his own, pulling a gun on Paul and telling him he's now blackmailing the couple for room and board. Hubert's entry into the domestic drama between Paul and Stanley is odd but even stranger is the fact that the next day, Hubert and Paul seem totally okay and discuss Stanley as if he was their wayward son. Additionally, Paul seems at ease with being dressed as Martha in this scene, and there's almost a family sitcom-feel to the entire thing. It doesn't last long, however, as Hubert is seen rifling through every drawer in the house, looking for money or drugs, a few scenes later. When Paul comes back inside and catches him in the act, Hubert runs out of the house and right into the pregnant Mrs. Adams from across the street, who is crushed under his fall. Paul chases Hubert onto a golf course and shoots him; meanwhile Stanley takes Mrs. Adams to the shed while she pleads for him to save her baby and then dies. Stanley then decides to use Paul's knife to cut the baby out of her dead body

Alma (Marty Cordova) coaxes Stanley (Wayne Crawford).

to save it, a move that surprises even Paul as he walks in and finds Stanley cradling the newborn gently. Paul, undoubtedly in panic mode at this point, insists they leave the baby on Vicki's doorstep, ditch Mrs. Adams' body somewhere, and make a run for it. The two eventually find themselves in an old movie studio where Stanley tells Paul he's ready to stop running. Finally feeling the ultimate betrayal, Paul snaps and the couple have their final showdown.

A big component to what makes *Sometimes Aunt Martha* so engaging is that it seems to be crossing into multiple genres at once: a gay melodrama tucked into a crime movie or a lovers-on-the-run story by way of the pastel splatter films of Herschell Gordon Lewis. Yet the relationship between Paul and Stanley is the most interesting puzzle you're compelled to solve while watching the film. A nuanced gay relationship on-screen in the 1970s seems fresh and forward-thinking yet there are a lot of unanswered questions about who these individuals are to each other that will provide tons of post-watch analysis. Unfortunately, little is known about the director Thomas Casey. He worked on a handful of exploitation films in the late 1960s before making *Sometimes Aunt Martha* and penned the notoriously bizarre *Flesh Feast*, best known as the actress Veronica Lake's last on-screen appearance. Yanka Mann, who plays Mrs. Adams in *Sometimes Aunt Martha* also appeared in *Flesh Feast* as did Brad F. Grinter, a Florida cult legend (he appears at the end of *Sometimes Aunt Martha* as a police officer). William Kerwin, another Florida exploitation mainstay and star of the Herschell Gordon Lewis classic *Blood Feast*, makes a brief, uncredited appearance as a detective. And while Wayne Crawford (Stanley) went on to have a long career in the movies, *Sometimes Aunt Martha* appears to be Abe Zwick's (Paul) sole acting credit.

Genre-ly Speaking

Florida's exploitation film industry can be traced back to at least the late 1950s with the "nudist camp" films (also known as "nudie cuties") of Doris Wishman and the filmmaking/producer duo of Herschell Gordon Lewis and David F. Friedman. Lewis, who is arguably the most famous director in the milieu, would make his pioneering gore film *Blood Feast* there in 1962 and would continue his string of Florida-set movies until his death in 2016. For more cinema from the Sunshine State, check out:

Nude on the Moon (1961)

Blood Feast (1962)

The Monster of Camp Sunshine or How I Learned to Stop Worrying and Love Nature (1964)

Two Thousand Maniacs! (1964)

She-Devils on Wheels (1968)

Scream Baby Scream (1969)

Flesh Feast (1970)

Zaat (1971)

Frogs (1972)

Blood Freak (1972)

Children Shouldn't Play with Dead Things (1972)

Miss Leslie's Dolls (1973)

Deathdream (1974)

THE BABY

USA, 1973 • COLOR, 84 MINUTES

Ruth Roman as the protective Mrs. Wadsworth

DIRECTOR: Ted Post   **SCREENPLAY:** Abe Polsky
STARRING: Anjanette Comer (Ann Gentry), Ruth Roman (Mrs. Wadsworth),
Marianna Hill (Germaine Wadsworth), Susanne Zenor (Alba Wadsworth),
David Mooney (Baby)

The term "exploitation film" has a basic meaning, which is a film that has elements that can be easily exploited to make a quick buck. As such, most exploitation films are designed to titillate, shock, and often go beyond what is considered tasteful by reasonable standards. Ted Post's *The Baby* is, on the surface, a truly bizarre exploitation movie. In it, a grown man lives the life of a toddler to the surprise of virtually no one, and in fact, his stunted existence is both constantly and fiercely protected by every person he comes across. The heated debate over whether he suffers from a developmental disability or has simply been conditioned by his revenge-fueled mother to act like a baby is discussed by certain characters but never actually resolved. And there's the twist ending that's so out of left field, it might make a viewer question why or how this movie was released (especially from a modern lens; politically correct, this film is not). But even as strange as the details are, *The Baby* is a surprisingly well made film, competently acted, and despite its PG rating, is never, ever boring. It's a true oddity even within the ranks of cult cinema, which is saying a lot, with just enough shock and awe to melt minds without the bitter aftertaste of pure exploitation.

Written by the screenwriter/producer Abe Polsky, known for the biker flick *The Rebel Rousers* (1970), the drive-in curiosity *Brute Corps* (1971), and *The Gay Deceivers*, a late '60s comedy about two straight men who pass as queer to dodge the draft, it allegedly took some convincing to get veteran director Ted Post to sign up for *The Baby*.

Post was best known for his television output where he worked on shows such as *Gunsmoke* and *The Twilight Zone*, and the feature films *Hang 'Em High* (1968) and *Beneath the Planet of the Apes* (1970). As he was already well established in his career and nowhere near the end, making a film like *The Baby* was an interesting choice, to say the least. Post considered the material too dark at first but eventually accepted the job; one could wonder how this movie would have turned out in less capable hands. Another Hollywood veteran, Ruth Roman, also signed up for *The Baby*. Roman had already made the transition to television after her studio career ended in the late 1950s, and she took the role as family

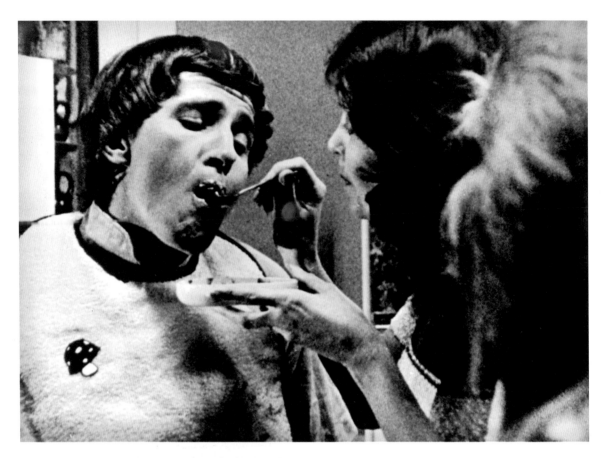

matriarch Mrs. Wadsworth. *The Baby* would effectively launch a second act in genre films for the former classic Hollywood star.

Mrs. Wadsworth is the single mother of three grown children: sisters Germaine and Alba and the only son, whom the family simply calls Baby. A social worker named Ann Gentry, still grieving the loss of her husband (and currently living with his mother), is sent to the home of the Wadsworth family and quickly discovers Baby has the stature of a grown man yet sleeps in a giant crib,

FROM TOP: The Baby (David Mooney) is fed by a social worker. • A victim is thrown into a homemade pit.

wears diapers and baby clothes, and crawls and coos, just like an infant. Following the visit, the Wadsworth ladies become more protective of Baby and suspicious of Ann's interference. Meanwhile, they often lock him in closets and shock him with a cattle prod when he misbehaves. Ann suspects Baby isn't intellectually disabled and that his mother is purposely infantilizing him as a general revenge on men, and a custody battle erupts between Ann and the Wadsworths. In her desperation to save this man, she plans to kidnap Baby, going against all the rules of her professional training. The final acts of the movie see the two parties in full showdown mode over the fate of Baby, with a true OMG ending that none of the previous minutes of the film would have predicted.

Even if we're never clear about any of their real intentions during the film, the women of *The Baby* are all a delight to watch. Ruth Roman as Mrs. Wadsworth is a wise, tough mama bear, reminiscent of Joan Crawford in a mid-career movie like *Johnny Guitar*. Marianna Hill and Susanne Zenor as the young, hip Wadsworth daughters are the willing henchwomen, ready to do their mother's bidding at any moment. The perfect encapsulation of this comes during what is arguably one of the most disturbing, outrageous scenes of the film where an adult female babysitter (Erin O'Reilly) has arrived to watch Baby while the three Wadsworth women go out. To their utter horror, they return to find the sitter breastfeeding Baby in his room. It's unclear if this bizarre act is being done out of care or if something more sinister is afoot; needless to say, Mrs. Wadsworth and her daughters

proceed to beat her senseless, right in front of Baby. The babysitter is not the only one with questionable motives: Anjanette Comer is haunting as Ann, and her slow turn from the film's protagonist to something more morally ambiguous will have you on the edge of your seat. *The Baby*'s unique take on motherhood comes right at the height of the women's liberation movement and makes for a strange yet entertaining 1970s cult film.

OMG Moment

In a movie filled with memorable scenes, one often cited as a favorite is the party sequence at the Wadsworth house. The party is actually a birthday celebration for Baby but includes all adults, the majority of them hippies, bikers, and other rough customers. As you would expect, the event is a rollicking romp filled with sex, drugs, and rock and roll, all while Baby crawls around on the floor in between partygoers. At one point, the babysitter from the harrowing breastfeeding scene is actually shown mingling at the party. After the beatdown she experienced from the Wadsworth women, it's hard to understand why she would have been invited to Baby's birthday party (and it's never addressed in the film). Perhaps an off-camera reconciliation happened? We will never know.

FLESHPOT ON 42ND STREET

USA, 1973 • COLOR, 87 MINUTES

Old friends Cherry Lane (Neil Flanagan) and Dusty Cole (Laura Cannon) catch up.

DIRECTOR: Andy Milligan   **SCREENPLAY:** Andy Milligan
STARRING: Laura Cannon (Dusty Cole), Neil Flanagan (Cherry Lane),
Harry Reems (Bob), Paul Matthews (Jimmie), Richard Towers (Tony)

By the 1920s, cinema had already begun its transformation into being a widely popular and powerful medium. But as its public consumption increased, so did scrutiny over what should and shouldn't be allowed on-screen. A number of scandals involving murder, drug use, and illicit sex had rocked major Hollywood stars and studios of the time, causing public outcry from groups wanting to boycott films they deemed immoral and giving rise to several proposed censorship bills from legislators. Politician William H. Hays was hired to help clean up the scandals and he presented a list of "Don'ts" and "Be Careful's" to the film industry in 1927. The guidance was largely ignored until June 1934, when Hays appointed journalist Joseph Breen, who established the Production Code Administration. The PCA required that all films obtain approval from the board before release, setting in motion a system that dictated what couldn't be shown on-screen for the next few decades—including references to sex and miscegenation. However, by 1973, when *Fleshpot on 42nd Street* was released, sex was on everyone's minds and on screens across the country.

The 1960s breakdown of the studio system and the Hays Code that had kept nudity and gratuitous mentions of sex off the screen allowed directors like Russ Meyer, Andy Milligan, and Joseph W. Sarno to cut their teeth directing "nudie cuties" and other sexploitation films that found their audience at grindhouse theaters. Milligan's *Fleshpot on 42nd Street*, alternatively titled *Girls on 42nd Street*, is one such movie, and one of the few remaining titles from his repertoire

that's still in circulation and hasn't been considered lost. The film itself is simple enough, drawing audiences into the exotic world of sex work and highlighting the complications endured by sex workers who actively engage in the profession.

Fleshpot on 42nd Street was released during the height of the "porno chic" era or the Golden Age of Porn, when X-rated films were being watched by mainstream audiences. The porno *Deep Throat* had just made waves and broken records the year before, and the Mitchell brothers' *Behind the Green Door* was on its way to becoming one of the most successful X-rated films after its 1972 release. Pornographic films were receiving red-carpet premieres, write-ups in *Rolling*

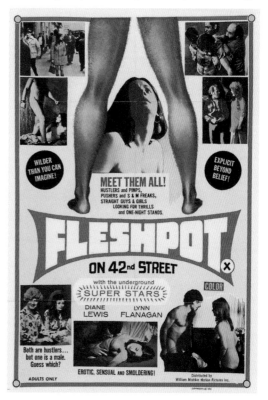

FROM LEFT: Dusty goes out on the once wild streets of 42nd Street. •
Dusty attempts to get money in whatever way she can.

Stone and the *New York Times*, references on late-night talk shows, and a mere year later, "Deep Throat" would become the well-known code name of a whistleblower who reported Richard Nixon's wrongdoings to journalists Carl Bernstein and Bob Woodward. Harry Reems, star of *Deep Throat*, stars alongside Laura Cannon under a pseudonym in *Fleshpot*.

Fleshpot spans roughly forty-eight hours with New York City sex worker Dusty, a character that initially serves as an anti-hero of sorts who feels confined by her current boyfriend's rules for living in his house. Dusty explains that she isn't cut out for office work but feels unfulfilled staying at home and being domesticated. Frustrated with being boxed in, Dusty steals a few items from his home and splits, selling what she can and turning tricks for money. Not averse to sex work, Dusty teams up with an old friend and hustling partner, a drag queen named Cherry

who takes Dusty in as a roommate. The two gallivant around the city over the next two days, turning tricks, bonding, and discovering ugly truths about each other. Meanwhile, the possibility of unconditional love arises for Dusty, a prospect that could turn her whole world upside. But will happiness and stability be her future?

Milligan had made dozens of underground films rife with sex, exposing aspects of society that had previously been considered the dregs. Prostitution, gay sex, nudity, uncouth language, and foul-mouthed offensiveness made him the king of the underground film and *Fleshpot on 42nd Street*, though made toward the end of his filmography, is no different. It carries the same hallmarks of pornography and was initially released as one, alongside a version that censored the hardcore sex scenes. Viewing this edgy classic will likely be a jarring experience for most filmgoers today, even the staunchest cult movie fan. This film was made for a particular and very small subsection of the public, not the masses. This is its charm and its strength. It's an examination of a concealed world operating in the fringes outside mainstream society, and from that artistic bird's-eye view alone, it's a captivating watch.

Fleshpot on 42nd Street doesn't possess the glitz and glamour of its cinematic counterparts but frankly resembles the quick and dirty stag-like films shown in cheap adult movie theaters or traded among collectors in a pre-internet world. It's not a pretty or aesthetically appealing film, but that doesn't mean that Milligan lacks a taut cinematic eye. Despite its cheap film stock and low-grade quality, Milligan's career masterpiece is surprisingly delicate when it needs to be, framing Dusty sweetly and intimately when she's presenting herself as such, then tense and thrilling when the action calls for it. The editing is tight and impressive.

Fleshpot on 42nd Street serves as a snapshot of a rapidly changing New York City and America at large, where social norms were being pushed to the edge as the post-hippie free love, gay rights, and feminist movements were taking hold. Dusty isn't punished for her work or her love of sex. She's a sexually liberated woman with no qualms about what she does, although she's more than aware of how others may judge her because of her work. While *Fleshpot* was a dime a dozen in its heyday, it's a rarity that manages to be reflective of the time and place it focuses on. Adult star Fred Lincoln perhaps summed it up best in an interview with the Rialto Report when he said "[*Fleshpot on 42nd Street*] is not really a porn film. . . . It's more like a Cassavettes [*sic*] film. I went to see it when it came out, and I thought it was art."

FRIGHT CLUB

For some of us, there's nothing more pleasurable than feeling a chill down the spine or the hairs rising on the back of our neck from a good old-fashioned cinematic scare. This chapter includes some of our fright favorites throughout the 1960s, '70s, and '80s as seen on TCM Underground. These late-twentieth-century titles feature the creeps, the jitters, and some memorable figures in the horror genre. Graveyards and the living dead are around every corner here, providing some alternative viewpoints on living by a cemetery or being a vampire. We also enter into the depths of hell with two examples that couldn't be more different, despite their apparent similarities. In fact, our Fright Club list could make for a series of intriguing double features that explore folklore, the occult, and the weakness of the flesh. Enter if you dare.

BLACULA

USA, 1972 • COLOR, 93 MINUTES

Vonetta McGee and William Marshall

DIRECTOR: William Crain **SCREENPLAY:** Joan Torres, Raymond Koenig
STARRING: William Marshall (Prince Mamuwalde/Blacula), Vonetta McGee
(Luva/Tina), Denise Nicholas (Michelle), Thalmus Rasulala (Dr. Gordon
Thomas), Gordon Pinsent (Lt. Jack Peters)

In the early 1970s, the B-film production company American International Pictures wanted to make a Black version of the classic *Dracula* story. Movies based on the famous vampire were having a resurgence thanks to the Gothic horror output of London's Hammer Film Productions, who released several starring the British actor Christopher Lee starting in the late 1960s. The desire to appeal to Black audiences was a part of AIP's overall formula, which also included action, sex appeal, and new, exciting takes on old stories in order to spark the interests of young people. AIP executive Samuel Arkoff was approached by a director named William Crain, who had just begun his career in television after graduating from UCLA's renowned film program. Crain was interested in directing for AIP, and especially for a Black character, though he hoped he could make *Blacula* more in line with standard horror fare, and less with the exploitation pictures the company was known for.

Crain's first step was hiring the classically trained Shakespearean actor William Marshall for the lead. Marshall had learned his trade in New York City, both at the Actors Studio and with the famous acting teacher Sanford Meisner, before beginning his career in such theater productions as *Carmen Jones*, *Peter Pan*, and *Othello*. Tall with a commanding bass voice, Marshall would not only cut an imposing figure but would also lend a suave, debonair energy to the notorious monster. Marshall would be an essential component to the film's success and would reprise his role in its sequel *Scream Blacula Scream* just a few years later.

Blacula begins in the year 1780 as Mamuwalde (Marshall), an African prince sent by the elders of his nation, and his wife, Luva (McGee), meet with the notorious Count Dracula in his castle. The couple are seeking his help to end the barbaric transatlantic slave trade, and the count is fast to list his reasons why he does not agree. He then insults Mamuwalde and Luva before a fight breaks out among the Prince and Dracula's servants, ending in Mamuwalde being bitten by the bloodsucker. Dracula deems Mamuwalde "Blacula" for all eternity, burying him in a coffin and sealing it (and Luva, left to die) inside a crypt in his castle.

Blacula strikes a pose.

FROM TOP: Blacula exiting the bedroom • Blacula, master of seduction

Cut to modern day, where an interracial gay couple named Bobby and Billy have just purchased the Count's estate, including the old coffin left in the crypt. Upon opening it, they stir Blacula from his sleep and become his very first victims. At the subsequent funeral for Bobby, Blacula notices that one of the mourners named Tina looks exactly like his late wife, Luva, and he becomes obsessed with reuniting with her. Tina's sister Michelle (Nicholas) comes to her rescue one night as Blacula follows her home. On the way to Tina's apartment, Blacula is accidentally hit by a cab driver named Juanita (played by the classic singer/actress Ketty Lester), and she becomes his second kill. Michelle's boyfriend, Dr. Gordon Thomas, a doctor working for the Los Angeles Police Department, inspects both Bobby and Juanita's corpses and starts to believe their deaths have something to do with vampirism. Meanwhile, Blacula finally catches up with Tina, who has now grown to enjoy his company. She slowly begins to fall in love with him, even after he's revealed his true identity to her. As more of Blacula's victims are presumed dead, they begin to reanimate as the undead, and a final, epic showdown occurs between the LAPD and the notorious vampire.

In a film made by a Black director and featuring a Black cast, perhaps it is unsurprising that issues of race constantly arise in *Blacula*, and not just in the first minutes of the film when Blacula is cursed by the bigoted, pro-slavery Count Dracula. In the many scenes featuring Dr. Thomas, his frustrations with his (mostly) white colleagues in the department have to do with convincing his white supervisor Lt. Peters to take the (mostly) Black victims in his case seriously. As he is the only character with any working knowledge of vampire lore, he is often the only person in the film who knows what to do, especially in the final act of the film as the police begin to encircle Blacula. (His character is not unlike Duane Jones's Ben, the hero in the classic horror film *Night of the Living Dead*.) Race also informs the remarks from the white morgue attendant (played by the classic character actor Elisha Cook Jr.) as he wheels Juanita out to be examined by

Dr. Thomas, commenting that Black women who drive taxi cabs are promiscuous. These moments would not only be revolutionary within the scope of cult cinema until this point, but they also resonated with the Black audiences who arrived in droves to see the film. *Blacula* became a smash success for American International Pictures and kicked off a wave of Black horror films that would be released steadily throughout the 1970s.

OMG Moment

The score to *Blacula* was composed by the legendary music producer Gene Page, who had his hand in the arrangements for many famous artists including the Supremes, the Four Tops, and Barbra Streisand. However, the band featured in the actual film during the nightclub scenes was the Hues Corporation, a soul trio best known for their 1974 hit "Rock the Boat." Performing the song "There He Is Again," the group dons powder-blue outfits, giving an energetic performance (sounding just as good as recorded material, miraculously, without any microphones visibly present). However, it's the multiple close-ups of the thrusting pelvis of their female singer, Hubert Ann Kelley, that make the scene both memorable and slightly hilarious. And just when you think her dress will definitely be too short to cover her nether region, the camera slyly cuts away.

GANJA & HESS

USA, 1973 • COLOR, 112 MINUTES

Dr. Hess Green (Duane Jones) offers Ganja Meda (Marlene Clark) a drink.

DIRECTOR: Bill Gunn and Lawrence Jordan   **SCREENPLAY:** Bill Gunn
STARRING: Duane Jones (Dr. Hess Green), Marlene Clark (Ganja Meda),
Bill Gunn (George Meda), Sam L. Waymon (Rev. Luther Williams),
Leonard Jackson (Archie)

Bill Gunn didn't want to make a vampire film when first approached to do so by Kelly-Jordan Enterprises. It was 1972 and *Blacula* was close to being released, so producers wanted in on what was sure to be a novelty treat at the box office. Gunn took the $350,000 offered to him but instead of a down-the-line vampire flick, he made an art-house film about a man in spiritual crisis—and made him a vampire doctor for good measure. Gunn then added a romantic interest, creating a sumptuous journey that follows a couple attempting to deal with their own missteps and traumas while being vampires addicted to blood. A dazzling picturesque, existential drama with vampires as a second thought wasn't what his producers had in mind.

Gunn appears in the film as George Meda, a depressed, suicidal man struggling with mental health issues. One night while working alongside his colleague Dr. Hess Green, George has a mental breakdown and repeatedly stabs Hess. Thinking Hess is dead, George then commits suicide, unaware that his actions have created a vampire as the dagger he used to stab Hess is an ancient Mayan relic that has cursed its victim with eternal life and a thirst for blood. The story is told in three parts—Victim, Survival, and Letting Go—with Part III serving as the film's main centerpiece and featuring the entrance of Ganja, George's estranged wife, who, in her search for her missing husband, falls in love with Hess. The two embark on a whirlwind romance and marry after Ganja discovers Hess's secret. But the sins of the flesh soon affect their lovers' paradise and Hess's addiction grows deeper, as does his search for a spiritual connection.

Ganja & Hess marked only the second on-screen appearance for Duane Jones, who had made his debut a few years prior in George A. Romero's groundbreaking horror film *Night of the Living Dead* (1968). *Ganja & Hess* also marked the second picture that Gunn directed, but the first to be released. A New York theater–trained actor, Gunn was known for his playwriting and acting skills, and he had scored a hit when he wrote the screenplay for Hal Ashby's *The Landlord* (1970). Marlene Clark had a number of credits to her name by the time *Ganja & Hess* was released, but her stunning performance as the cool, devilish, and stylish Ganja Meda is without a doubt her most well known. Also featured in the cast is Leonard Jackson of *Five on the Black Hand Side* and later *Car Wash* (1976).

Ganja struggles with existence as a vampire.

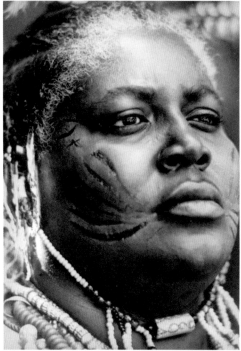

Ganja & Hess premiered at the 1973 Cannes Film Festival and received glowing reviews from critics, but audiences didn't connect with it, and the production company recut the film beyond recognition in hopes that it would increase box-office returns. As many critics have noted, *Ganja & Hess* was ahead of its time. Following on the heels of Melvin Van Peebles's cinematic juggernaut *Sweet Sweetback's Baadasssss Song* (1971), *Ganja & Hess* was mistimed for the 1973 film market. *Blacula* was successful both at the box office and with critics a year prior, and the era of Blaxploitation had revved up by 1973, delivering low-budget but action-packed, easy-to-swallow films by the dozens. A psychological drama about existential and

FROM TOP: Archie (Leonard Jackson) falls victim. • A woman from Hess's dreams

spiritual crisis matched with addiction and masked by vampirism didn't have much of a chance under the circumstances.

Nevertheless, we're thrilled to recommend that this film get another look. It's simply electrifying in its originality and was handled expertly by everyone involved, including the director of photography, the costume designer, the set designer, and the composer. Together, these elements blend effortlessly to create lavish shots of Gothic-style decadence. Though the film isn't necessarily scary, Gunn has a knack for presenting uniquely framed scenes that encapsulate the essence of fear and anxiety, often constructing overhead, canted shots that make rooms feel slightly askew. In a particularly noteworthy shot, George and Hess talk outside in front of a large tree. George is drunk and sitting in Hess's tree, and we only see his feet dangling as a noose tied on the branch next to him hangs. Hess stands in front of the rope attempting to convince George not to kill himself because of the trouble it would bring Hess, having a Black man dead on his property. The scene is chilling to watch as the dangling feet and Hess's framed body in front of the rope elicit the very real fears of the world these men exist in, without vampires or folklore.

Complete with hallucinations and dream-like images running rampant throughout *Ganja & Hess*'s runtime, the film is a sumptuous treat of eye candy. It's a patient film that builds slowly but doesn't lose track of where it is or where it's going. Jones and Clark have fantastic chemistry together, and Jackson manages some of the most humorous moments in spite of his limited screen time. *Ganja & Hess* is an entertaining journey that manages to expand on the vampire folklore, as mirrors and sunshine are in abundance for the living dead, but crosses and bloodlust represent a much deeper and more poignant theme for these denizens of the undead.

Did You Know

Bill Gunn has had the distinct honor of being the second African American director in cinematic history backed by a Hollywood studio for his feature *Stop!* (1970). But the film was recut by Warner Bros. and shelved, never having an official release. Nevertheless, Gunn's legacy has expanded in the years after his 1989 death, with director Spike Lee calling him one of the most underappreciated filmmakers of our time. Lee remade *Ganja & Hess* in 2014 as *Da Sweet Blood of Jesus*. A talented but largely unrecognized actress, Marlene Clark is also gaining recognition today for her career. The model turned actress starred in a number of underground hits that prevented her from skyrocketing into notability. Her starring role in *Stop!* didn't see the light of day, and many of her featured roles are in films that have become cult classics that we personally adore, including *Putney Swope* (1969), *Night of the Cobra Woman* (1972), *Beware! The Blob* (1972), *The Beast Must Die* (1974), *Black Mamba* (1974), and *Switchblade Sisters* (1975).

HÄXAN

SWEDEN, 1922 • B&W/TINTED COLOR, 105 MINUTES

Satan (Benjamin Christensen) is fierce and ready to take souls as his agents.

DIRECTOR: Benjamin Christensen **SCREENPLAY:** Benjamin Christensen
STARRING: Maren Pedersen (Heksen/The Witch), Clara Pontoppidan
(Nonne/Nun), Elith Pio (Heksedommer/Witch Judge), Oscar Stribolt
(Graabroder/Doctor [The Fat Monk]), Tora Teje (En hysterisk kvinde/
Modern Hysteric [The Kleptomaniac]), John Andersen (Chief Inquisitor),
Benjamin Christensen (Djævlen/The Devil)

Feature-length films were still relatively novel in 1922, but the art form had practically cemented its narrative structure by the early 1920s, a structure that hasn't changed much one hundred years later. Films generally possessed a linear storytelling model, a consistent storyteller, a mostly identifiable genre, and a clear boundary between fiction and nonfiction. While a number of directors in the silent era chose to make films that distorted these norms, Swedish director Benjamin Christensen's *Häxan* is one of the films that made an unmistakable mark on cinema by deconstructing its conventions to create a work that remains remarkably original and breathtaking a century later.

Inspiration for *Häxan* struck Christensen when he found *Malleus Maleficarum* in a bookshop. The fifteenth-century book detailed ways for identifying and "neutralizing" witches. Christensen then spent two years researching the history of witchcraft, reading several books and gathering sources for a film. He wanted to make something new rather than a straightforward adaptation of what he had been reading. The result is an outstanding blend of documentary and fictitious reenactments cobbled together in a pre-formative video essay format that chronicles the origins around the folklore of witches. Furthermore, the film goes on to expose the hypocrisies and crimes of the inquisition during the thirteenth century when witch trials swept through Europe, killing scores of mostly women along with children and men before the mass hysteria ended. Christensen rounds out the film by connecting the dots to convey how the tragedies of the past affect the present.

Häxan is divided into seven parts. Most of the film moves forward and backward through time, as well as in and out of narrative story to detail the history of witchcraft, the ensuing trials, and disturbing examples of torture and hysteria. Our narrative tale follows an elderly beggar who is falsely accused of being a witch by an elite family distraught that the man of the house has fallen ill seemingly out of nowhere. A member of the family insists that a witch must be the reason and a local folk doctor confirms this supposed fact. They present the accusation to the Catholic inquisition, which proceeds to take sadistic pleasure in torturing the woman for her confessions. This leads to more accusations, more torture, and conviction from the inquisition that Satan is openly and actively rebelling against the holy order on Earth.

Framed through a Gothic-era aesthetic, much of the film's creepiest moments are felt through mise-en-scene and blocking.

Nuns just want to have fun.

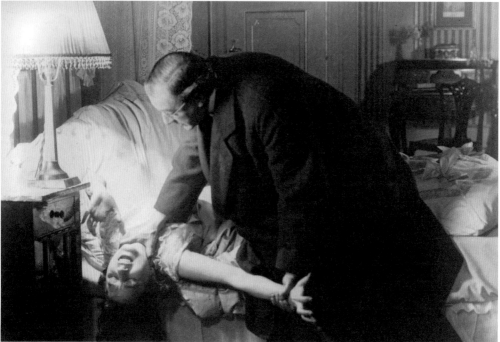

FROM TOP: The Satanic ritual requires a sacrifice. • Hysteria affects more than women.

Christensen applied an array of special effects in-camera and on set, resulting in a silent film that feels modern in its visual style. Stop-motion animation, reverse projection, practical makeup, puppetry, and forced perspectives are all paired expertly with tight close-ups, detailed backdrops, moving dioramas, and elaborate costume design to create an electric environment filled with tension, tragedy, and informative lessons on history. *Häxan* features some spectacular editing that at times brings levity to grim moments, such as when a fictitious retelling of a Satanic ceremony shows Satan vigorously churning butter with a phallic tool before the scene cuts abruptly to the priests' shocked, staring faces.

At times *Häxan* feels like an anthropological study of how societies crippled by fear respond to the ever-changing and harsh environment around them. Christensen boldly presents ways in which blatant misogynic actions inflicted pain and suffering mostly on women during these trials. *Häxan* is self-aware as a documentary, allowing Christensen to impose his thoughts and perspectives into the narrative through the film's title cards. He frequently peels back the curtain, narratively speaking, to reveal information about his filmmaking process, such as when his assistant wants to try on the real-life torture objects that the film displays.

This proto-feminist, anticlerical focus was widely condemned upon *Häxan*'s release. The film was banned in many countries outside Sweden for decades in part because of this, and due to its use of (light) nudity, its sexual allusions, and its representation of Satan. Ultimately, the film proved too ahead of its time as it confused critics and did little to impress the public. It was rereleased in 1941 but gained its cult status in 1967 when thirty minutes of the film were shaved off and it was released as *Witchcraft Through the Ages*. Today, this cinematic curiosity is continuously celebrated in artists' circles across the world, with screenings in festivals accompanied by original scores. Though Christensen made over a dozen more films, worked for a brief time at MGM, and starred in a handful of films, including the seminal gay-themed Carl Theodor Dreyer picture *Michael*, he never made another picture that had the lasting impact of *Häxan*.

Genre-ly Speaking

Looking for more recommendations for occult-inspired films featuring Satanism, witchcraft, and alchemy? Here are a few of our cult favorites:

Black Sunday (1960)

City of the Dead (aka *Horror Hotel*) (1960)

Baba Yaga (aka *Kiss Me, Kill Me*) (1973)

The Wicker Man (1973)

Suspiria (1977)

Prince of Darkness (1987)

Mirror Mirror (1990)

The House of the Devil (2009)

The Witch (2015)

A Dark Song (2016)

JIGOKU

JAPAN, 1960 • COLOR, 101 MINUTES

The simple and effective use of set design and practical effects

DIRECTOR: Nobuo Nakagawa **SCREENPLAY:** Nobuo Nakagawa, Ichirō Miyagawa
STARRING: Shigeru Amachi (Shirō Shimizu), Utako Mitsuya (Yukiko/Sachiko),
Yōichi Numata (Tamura), Hiroshi Hayashi (Gōzō Shimizu), Jun Ōtomo (Ensai
Taniguchi), Akiko Yamashita (Kinuko), Kiyoko Tsuji (Kyōichi's Mother), Fumiko
Miyata (Mrs. Yajima), Torahiko Akira Nakamura (Professor Yajima)

If you're ever having a day that you just can't make the best of—maybe your car won't start, maybe you're running late, or you just got fired—whatever it is, get out of your funk by watching *Jigoku*. By the film's end you may be scratching your head in puzzlement, but at least you'll recognize that your day is nowhere near as bad as lead character Shirō's, whose day is without a doubt, hands-down, worse than yours. Directed by Nobuo Nakagawa, *Jigoku* is a mind trip into the dark recesses of hell. It's a hodgepodge, kitchen-sink movie that's part Ingmar Bergman, part Roger Corman, part Douglas Sirk, and part Salvador Dali, adding up to a delectably morbid cinematic feat that explores hell with an insatiable appetite not seen in art since Dante's *Inferno*.

Shirō, the poor soul, just can't catch a break. His life was presumably good until that one night when the incident happened. A college student with good looks and a promising future, Shirō gets roped into riding home with his friend and schoolmate Tamura, who's the obvious rebel out to get his kicks and damn whoever is in the way. On their ride home, Tamura suggests Shirō take an unexpected turn, leading to a hit-and-run and a cascading series of unfortunate events that turns Shirō's life upside down.

The two are unknowingly hunted down by the lover and mother of the now dead passerby, and eventually Shirō finds himself near the depths of hell caught in limbo with a myriad of strange characters. Is salvation possible for Shirō? Can he escape the eternal torture of hell to prove his humanity? Spoiler alert: the results are fuzzy at best, but it's the

journey we embark on that's the fascinating ride, not the destination.

Jigoku was released in 1960, during an important time for Japanese cinema. Japan's creative output had been regulated by foreign forces since the aftermath of World War II, making films that focused on sex, violence, and politics a rarity during the 1940s and 1950s. Japan's cinematic reputation was instead largely dominated by the works of Akira Kurosawa, who primarily made historically driven samurai period pieces. By the end of the 1950s, the American occupation of Japan ended, allowing the directors of the nation to freely explore more sensational stories about crime and horror.

Jigoku director Nobuo Nakagawa had been a prolific filmmaker behind the camera since 1934 but hit a successful stride while at Toho and Shintoho Co. Ltd., two of the country's six major film studios. During the 1950s, he became primarily known for making "kaidan" movies, or films focusing on strange, bewitching, horrific elements, and *Jigoku* perfectly embodies that style. However, by the time he made *Jigoku*, it proved to be the final film for Shintoho studios, which was under financial collapse and filed for bankruptcy a year later.

Though it wasn't universally embraced at the time of its release, *Jigoku* managed to earn its cult status as a precursor to a later genre of film. Had the thriller been made in the late 1960s, it would likely have been lost to a dozen or so films capturing psychedelic, trippy visuals on celluloid. Nevertheless, like with so many underground classics, audiences of the time weren't ready for Nakagawa's artistic assault on the senses or his bleak

The Sinner of Hell in the heads of Satan's minions • **OPPOSITE:** Shirō (Shigeru Amachi) struggles to save the ones he loves in hell.

view of the afterlife found in the screenplay he co-wrote with Ichirō Miyagawa. But the sleeper did find its audience as the years went by, hitting perhaps its most popular peak in the 1990s during the global popularity of a new generation of Japanese horror.

Jigoku doesn't feel made for a global, English-speaking audience. It's an esoteric, philosophical, and religious tale steeped in cultural reference points and iconography. It doesn't hand-hold audiences into understanding why or what is happening, nor does it explain the idiosyncratic nature of what unfolds on-screen. And yet, there's a poetic fluidity running through the film that has recognizable iconography for outsiders to latch onto. *Jigoku* is a cinematic feat, its impressive use of in-camera editing techniques makes this already cerebral fever dream into the stuff of nightmares. While it may have pulled inspiration from films like *A Page of Madness* (1926), *Jigoku*'s unique aesthetic and very existence had an impact on such later psychological horror entries as *In the Mouth of Madness* (1994), *Jacob's Ladder* (1990), *Ringu* (1998), and its American remake *The Ring* (2002).

OMG Moment

Shirō's descent into hell is a strange and frightening sequence of the film that's unexpected and jarring. As the levels of hell are explained to the unfortunate souls who find themselves there, audiences are treated to a barrage of terrifying, outlandish sequences. Souls are judged by their earthly sins and punished accordingly in gruesome ways: sawed in half, dismembered, flayed, poked, or prodded amidst the flames of eternal damnation. Despite its macabre feel, it's surprisingly creative and fascinating to watch. Though it's tamer than most violence depicted in films today, the sequence still manages to be surprising in its depiction of nightmarish imagery and will likely inspire a new take for a Halloween costume.

LET'S SCARE JESSICA TO DEATH

USA, 1971 • COLOR, 89 MINUTES

Jessica (Zohra Lampert) longs for comfort.

DIRECTOR: John D. Hancock **SCREENPLAY:** John D. Hancock, Lee Kalcheim

STARRING: Zohra Lampert (Jessica), Barton Heyman (Duncan),

Kevin O'Connor (Woody), Gretchen Corbett (The Girl),

Alan Manson (Sam Dorker), Mariclare Costello (Emily)

Mental illness as the catalyst for horror didn't get its start in the 1970s. From *Gaslight* (1944) to *The Innocents* (1961) and on to *The Babadook* (2014), people dealing with horrific situations brought on by psychosis, or the perceived notion of psychosis, is a tale as old as time in the horror genre. So, *Let's Scare Jessica to Death*'s theme of mental illness isn't a particularly unique element, but the surrounding layers of the film are. In the film, Jessica is newly released from a psychiatric treatment facility and heading with her husband and friend to recuperate and start life anew in a Connecticut farmhouse. Immediately, Jessica notices that things are askew when she begins envisioning strange happenings and people in the area surrounding her home. But will anyone believe her, or are these images just figments of a mind that once again is untethered from reality?

What makes *Let's Scare Jessica to Death* such an intriguing surprise is that it spent so long buried in the rubble of cinematic obscurity. On its release in 1971, the film confused critics and despite a VHS release in the 1980s, it slipped into virtual obscurity until its 2006 DVD release, when a new audience embraced its haunting, eerie atmosphere and the strong performance of Zohra Lampert as Jessica. Its legacy undoubtedly suffered in part because its marketing misrepresented the film's contents. The original poster art promised skeleton bones and wielding knives, leading audiences to expect related thrills, only to realize they are merely symbolic images of what's occurring in this film.

Jessica is obsessed with death, but that's not the story line here; it's merely a subtextual examination of her character. Projecting a childlike innocence in her performance, Lampert's Jessica prances through graveyards finding beauty in the art of gravestone rubbings, in which she places paper over gravestones and rubs graphite over the paper, saving the images for wall art. This young wife may be morbid, but she's not despondent. She's a gentle soul with a sweet nature emboldened by Lampert's tender performance that conveys all Jessica's fears of losing her grasp on reality and disappointing those around her. Jessica's friends and loved ones seem to possess only the tiniest bit of empathy for her, growing more detached and frustrated by her fragile state as they spend more time alone together in the house. But their behavior is also affected by a strange drifter squatting at the home when they arrive, whom they invite to stay.

Let's Scare Jessica to Death is unique in being a hippie-era horror film that shows the dark side of free love and the good Samaritan vibes of the movement that swept through late-1960s America, a time when wearing flowers in one's hair was considered a revolutionary act of protest and young people were exploring new ways of interacting socially. The hippie trio, Jessica, Duncan, and Woody, finds themselves at the crux of this great divide when the small-town community reacts with hostility to their long hair and their trendy vehicle of a hearse. Their house is meant to be their comfort zone, but it immediately proves the contrary. Jessica notices strange remnants of objects in the house, memorabilia of a sinister past, and she starts seeing people and deathly visions around her. What's worse, no one is willing or able to

Jessica is on the run from her demons. **OPPOSITE:** A desperate Jessica is in need of help

believe her, making her stress almost palpable as the audience is aware—or at least we *think* we know—that these visions are indeed real. While the story shifts into the territory of vampirism, its blood-sucking theme is not lost on the overall arc.

This marked director John Hancock's sophomore film, which he co-wrote with Lee Kalcheim during the decline of the hippie movement. *Let's Scare Jessica to Death* feels more like a critique of the era masquerading as a horror film. Other characters leech off Jessica's virtuous compassion, and she is never met with the same kindness or patience that she delivers. While her housemates take advantage of the notion of free love, they do so selfishly. Jessica can't seem to find her place in this new world, one that's outside an institution and away from the inner city, the very environment that drove her to a nervous breakdown, and she fears returning to it. But Jessica's fresh start is filled with uncertainty; even those she's supposed to trust may be untrustworthy, a predicament that makes this film a tense journey into madness from the very first scene to the end.

Genre-ly Speaking

The folk horror genre existed before the release of *Let's Scare Jessica to Death*, but it had only just been given a name, and at the time it only referred to Piers Haggard's *The Blood on Satan's Claw* (1971). Folk horror hit its stride in the 1970s and has since ballooned into a fully formed, beloved genre of horror that saw perhaps its biggest accolades yet with *Midsommar* (2019). Atmospheric and often set in rural surroundings, folk horror veered in a different direction from Gothic horror, in which the subgenre was rooted. Folk horror forgoes the castles, statues, ominous architecture, and lightning storms for small-town life, rustic homes, and shady neighbors (often affiliated with a cult or the occult), and it makes the serene lushness of outdoors feel sinister. The settings are geographically expansive—Nebraska for *Children of the Corn*, Scotland in the case of *The Wicker Man*, Australia for *Picnic at Hanging Rock*, Florida's countryside for *Jeepers Creepers*, the woods of Maryland for *The Blair Witch Project*—but regardless of locale, if it's rural, there's a local legend or mystery, and most of the action happens outside, you've found yourself in a folk horror.

THE BROOD

CANADA, 1979 • COLOR, 92 MINUTES

Frank (Art Hindle) stumbles on a deadly discovery.

DIRECTOR: David Cronenberg   **SCREENPLAY:** David Cronenberg

STARRING: Oliver Reed (Dr. Hal Raglan), Samantha Eggar (Nola Carveth),
Art Hindle (Frank Carveth), Henry Beckman (Barton Kelly),
Nuala Fitzgerald (Juliana Kelly), Cindy Hinds (Candice Carveth),
Susan Hogan (Ruth Mayer), Gary McKeehan (Mike Trellan)

Canadian writer-director David Cronenberg's name is synonymous with the body horror genre. Having made a name for himself with such unforgettable entries as *Scanners* (1981), *Videodrome* (1983), *The Fly* (1986), *Dead Ringers* (1988), and *Crash* (1996), Cronenberg has proven his cinematic expertise in exploring the malleability and destruction of the body in various ways. He made his feature directing debut in 1969 with *Stereo (Tile 3B of a CAEE Educational Mosaic)*, then scored two back-to-back hits with *Shivers* (1975) and *Rabid* (1977), both marking an impressive feat of becoming the highest-grossing films in Canada during their release.

Today, Cronenberg's career has established him as a revered and respected filmmaker, but in 1979, Cronenberg was still a newcomer, cutting his teeth making off-the-wall, unique horror films, thanks to the Canadian tax shelter (see Genre-ly Speaking, page 37). Commonly referred to as Canuxploitation, Cronenberg became one of the many directors that benefited from this era of Canadian filmmaking, and he quickly defined himself as an auteur of horror. Of all his fantastic contributions to the B-movie subset of films, 1979's *The Brood* is perhaps the most characteristic work in the director's oeuvre, refining how he views disease and the human body, along with the contradictions of the body's frailty and power.

The Brood exists in a reality where disease and trauma manifest with immediate real-world complications. Frank is a recently divorced single father taking care of his young daughter and working through the struggles of sharing custody with his mentally unstable ex-wife, Nola, who is undergoing controversial psychiatric care from Dr. Hal Raglan. The doctor practices a method that asks his patients to relive their traumas in ways that develop into physical symptoms, like sores and cancerous tumors on their

bodies. Frank begins noticing bruises on his daughter after she visits Nola, jump-starting a series of unusual events in which those close to Nola and her rage end up being killed by strange, dwarflike beings. Frank fights to discover the origins of these murders in order to keep his daughter safe, but his intentions may not have the effect he desires.

FROM TOP: Candice (Cindy Hines) is attacked by sinister beings. • Nola (Samantha Eggar) has a dangerous secret to reveal.

The Brood delivers unexpected scares and creeps that still hold up over forty years later. This is undoubtedly thanks to the talented creative team behind the scenes, including the makeup department, sound department, set design, and music by Howard Shore, who would go on to compose scores for most of Cronenberg's later films and win three Oscars for his work on *The Lord of the Rings* films. Cronenberg penned the screenplay for *The Brood* after enduring his own bitter divorce from his first wife and the ensuing custody battle for his daughter. He later admitted that the experience put him and his daughter through great turmoil.

The raw emotion that inspired Cronenberg makes *The Brood* a frightening and emotionally charged watch, aided by the strong performances of his stars. Cindy Hinds, in her film debut, is marvelous as the dejected, traumatized center of the Carveth family's downfall. She's heartbreaking to watch by the disturbing final act, as the gravity of the past few weeks and their effect on her psyche become apparent with her settling into a quiet lucidity and detachment. Cronenberg does a fantastic job contrasting Cindy's innocence with the chaotic and horrific events that surround her, such as when she plays with a flower, lost in thought while her father photographs images of her bruised back for his custody case. Samantha Eggar as Nola delivers an equally striking performance, channeling icy rage and grief when revelations about her own childhood abuse come to the forefront during her therapy sessions. These new feelings of anger and fear wreak havoc on Nola's family, causing the manifested beings to embark on a murderous rampage in a scene where Eggar performs with flamboyant flair, playing off classic star Oliver Reed with vigor.

Despite its serious subject matter, Cronenberg delivers a thriller that is equally food for thought and a great late-night spine tickler. Like most, if not all, of his films, it's unlike anything before it or during its era. Although many critics were revolted by the film at the time of its release, it was a box-office success, earning $5 million off its $1.5 million

budget and staying in circulation for well over a year later in Canada. Often overshadowed by Cronenberg's later and flashier films, *The Brood*'s influence is nonetheless apparent in a number of modern-day movies including *The Taking of Deborah Logan* (2014), *The Babadook* (2014), *Split* (2016), and *Under the Shadow* (2016).

WTF Moment

The Brood is filled with grotesque and graphic (though tastefully shot) moments, but its most notorious scenes feature Samantha Eggar's big reveal that (spoiler alert) she's the mother of the demonic-looking children who are killing at her bidding. While her husband attempts to distract her so that Dr. Hal can rescue Cindy from the clutches of the beings, Frank can't help but show his disgust when Nola lifts her dress to reveal a placenta on the outside of her body, as well as numerous other abnormalities of the flesh. She then lifts the sac to her mouth, tearing it open to give birth to a new creation of hate, which she proceeds to lick clean. It's an unsettling scene that will stay in your mind thanks to the creation of fantastic special effects by Allan Cotter.

THE HOUSE BY THE CEMETERY

ITALY, 1981 • COLOR, 86 MINUTES

The dead come to life.

DIRECTOR: Lucio Fulci **SCREENPLAY:** Elisa Briganti, Dardano Sacchetti,
Giorgio Mariuzzo, Lucio Fulci
STARRING: Catriona MacColl (Lucy Boyle), Paolo Malco (Dr. Norman Boyle), Ania
Pieroni (Ann, the Babysitter), Giovanni Frezza (Bob Boyle), Silvia Collatina (Mae
Freudstein), Dagmar Lassander (Laura Gittleson), Giovanni De Nava (Dr. Freudstein)

Italian director Mario Bava held sway over the Italian *giallo* genre that arose after his films *The Girl Who Knew Too Much* (1963) and *Blood and Black Lace* (1964). These murder mysteries and thrillers, produced largely in Italy at their apex, are noted for their hyper-stylized look, their violent nature, and their focus on a central female character who witnesses a murder but whose testimony is called into question. Throughout the late 1960s and into the 1970s, as the Spaghetti Western (as it crudely became known for being produced in Italy) fell out of favor with the public, Italian *giallo* and horror quickly took over as crowd-pleasers, nearly dominating the output of Italy's productions.

This movement in cinema was led by directors Lucio Fulci, Joe D'Amato, Umberto Ruggero Deodato, and Gualtiero Jacopetti. Fulci's name is likely unrecognizable to fans of earlier Italian cinema, but his name reigns supreme for fans of Italian horror or "splatter cinema," as he saw success and glory in his day, particularly with the release of *The House by the Cemetery*. Being primarily a horror film and not classified as a *giallo*, the film still has the blueprints of the genre. This potpourri of horror has got it all and is sure to send a shiver or two down your spine. Sinister kids? Check. Haunted house? Check. Creepy dolls? Yep! Bats? Why not? Ghosts? Of course. Zombies? Yes. And for good measure, the script throws in some fun subtext involving a questionable husband and mental instability.

The husband in question here is Dr. Norman Boyle, who moves his wife, Lucy, and his adolescent son, Bob, from New York City to the suburbs to live in the old home of a former

colleague for research. The money he'll be making for this short-term move is too good to pass up, but the house has a dubious history. For starters, it's nestled snugly in front of an old cemetery, and soon the family learns that not only did the former owner murder his wife and commit suicide, but dead bodies are buried beneath their feet and strange noises continually emerge from the home. Norman's wife just wants it all to go away and will do anything to stop the terror. Bob is discussing the matter with a new friend, a girl that only he can see, and she's constantly warning him not to stay in the house. "My parents won't listen," he tells her. "They do what they want." Naturally, theses odd occurrences and bumps

Mae (Silvia Collatina) looks on with uncertainty.

in the night increase and the horror intensifies as the family begins to uncover more difficult truths about their new home.

Giallo and Italian horror films predated the American slasher, and Fulci was known for his pioneering use of gory effects such as squibs and other viscous delights for splattering blood and guts. This practice earned Fulci his nickname "The Godfather of Gore," and The House by the Cemetery clearly showcases why with its attention to detail on throats being slashed, heads being cut off, body parts being stabbed, and an array of other gruesome dismemberments. These moments are sure to make the toughest stomachs churn, but that doesn't take away from the thrills and spooks the movie possesses aside from its gore. Walter Rizzati's haunting score has a way of inciting chills thanks to its intense stabbing synthesizers and a repetitive sequence that resembles the notoriously eerie chord known as "the devil's tritone." Together with strong

performances from its lead actors, particularly Giovanni Frezza, The House by the Cemetery's initial rocky start is absolved by the end.

The House by the Cemetery is a strong horror film, but we can't ignore the obviously fun and at times laughable garishness that makes it so endearing right from the beginning. Because the Italian film industry didn't build soundstages or wire their studios for sound, all vocalizations of characters were done in post-production. Watch any Italian film during this era and you'll giggle a few times at the jarring sound that doesn't always match the lips or the mood of a scene. Likewise, the convoluted screenplay works just enough to make loose sense, if you don't think about it too long. This is a film that invites you to sit back and enjoy the ride. Regardless, none of these cheesy elements takes away from a haunting experience that has a surprisingly daunting ending. Fulci's haunted house tale is scary and fun and one that should be revisited.

WTF Moment

There are plenty of moments to spark a jolt when watching *The House by the Cemetery*, but our favorite has got to be the bat attack. The buildup to this scene is wonderfully constructed. Norman is planning once and for all to prove that there's nothing to be afraid of in the locked basement, so he sets to work opening the rusted, sealed door that should have just been left alone. Bob comes home before the fun starts and the music builds. Lucy begins to feel uneasy that Bob has once again mentioned his friend that no one has seen. As Norman shows that he has found the key, a series of unsettling looks is shared among Norman, Lucy, and Ann. Norman proceeds to pry open the door as the music cuts to silence, letting the noise of the creaky lock squeak until it's open. Norman makes his way down the stairs only to be attacked by a bat. What appears harmless at first turns into a Tippi-Hedren-in-*The-Birds* level of attack, the bat refusing to let go until Norman has to resort to drastic measures to free himself. The scene is equal parts hilarious, shocking, and terrifying to watch play out.

A murder takes place in *The House by the Cemetery*.

REBELLION & YOUTH MOVEMENTS

To say that being a teenager is hard would be an understatement. We've all been there before and remember the acne, the heartbreak, the isolation, the anxiety, and the awkwardness of figuring out who we are. On top of that, we just wanted to be respected and feel accepted. Unfortunately, the world isn't always kind to teenagers, but thankfully the movies are. These films all focus on being young, rebellious, and coming of age in various ways; they cut to the heart of being youthful, wild, and free and present teenagers and young adults doing their best to figure it out with the tools they have. Whether by using music, cars, or sex, the youth in these films learn how to carve their own place in an often uncaring, condescending world. Buckle up and enjoy the joy ride.

FIVE ON THE BLACK HAND SIDE

USA, 1973 • COLOR, 96 MINUTES

Carl Franklin is son-in-law Marvin.

DIRECTOR: Oscar Williams **SCREENPLAY:** Charlie L. Russell

STARRING: Godfrey Cambridge (Godfrey Cambridge), Clarice Taylor (Mrs. Brooks), Leonard Jackson (Mr. Brooks), Virginia Capers (Ruby), Glynn Turman (Gideon), D'Urville Martin (Booker T.), Richard Williams (Preston), Ja'net DuBois (Stormy Monday), Tchaka Almoravids (Fun Loving), Carl Franklin (Marvin)

Another film that's often inaccurately dumped into the large bucket of 1970s Blaxploitation movies is *Five on the Black Hand Side*. This misjudged and overlooked drama is about as far from the label of Blaxploitation as *Citizen Kane* (1941) would be if it were labeled a mystery. Written by NAACP Award–winning writer Charlie L. Russell and based on his play of the same name, *Five on the Black Hand Side* is a love letter to Black culture and reflective of an open dialogue that was taking place in the community and still happening more than forty years later. Above all, it's a family drama that's reminiscent of the work of playwright Lorraine Hansberry but possesses a consistent quirky humor that sets it apart from its contemporaries. It holds firm in its modernity, to the point of being a precursor of liberated Black stories to come.

It follows the Brookses, a family of five living on the east side of New York. John Henry is the patriarch, leading the household with a sharp tongue and short fuse. His frustrated, mousy wife, Gladys, is on the verge of cracking, as she's had enough of his verbally abusive and domineering ways. Mrs. Brooks isn't the only family member walking on eggshells around Mr. Brooks. Their youngest son, Gideon, has returned home from college and is living on the roof of their apartment building since staying inside with his father has become too much. Their oldest son, Booker T., is dealing with conflicting political beliefs. On one hand, he wants to be a radical and change his name to a more African-inspired one, but he also sees the value in following in his father's footsteps and working within the system to get by, to Gideon's disappointment.

Their daughter, Ruby, just wants things to calm down before her upcoming wedding is destroyed by the family's various clashes. However, around the eve of Ruby's marriage to an Afrocentric-minded man named Marvin, the family dynamics ignite into an explosion of emotional, political, and sociological discourse, causing all to reassess themselves and their own personal beliefs.

It's unfortunate that this powerful film has been lost to the masses over the decades. Clearly unapologetic for its tone and general themes of Black power, *Five on the Black Hand Side* is more of a social picture than anything else. Its aim was obviously to spark a dialogue within the Black community, and

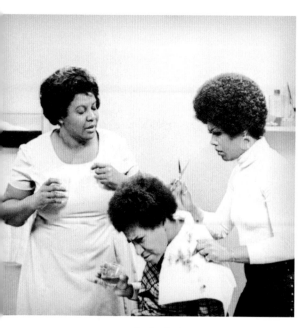

FROM LEFT: Clarice Taylor stars as Mrs. Brooks, undergoing a life-changing haircut with her friends. •
Two characters give each other five in the aptly titled film.

Russell felt indifferent about alienating general moviegoers. In an interview with *Black Drama*, he stated, "In *Five on the Black Hand Side* I tried to do two things, and that was raise the level of consciousness and to unify black people." The conversations within the film don't feel heavy-handed or preachy. They flow naturally through their characters, who in turn feel like self-realized humans engaging in the ideological milieu of the era. Everything from interracial dating and Afrocentrism to misogyny and self-actualization is up for discussion here. The entire film deftly softens the deep topics with some hilarious, offbeat moments of humor experienced from the opening scene when comedian Godfrey Cambridge appears as himself and gets into a fender bender in which he blames the stopped car

he hit for not signaling as opposed to the real culprit: his wandering eye.

Five on the Black Hand Side mostly feels like a sitcom and at times is reminiscent of an episode of the TV series *Good Times*, which was only a year away from being created. *Five on the Black Hand Side* is historically significant for heralding popular entertainment that would actively showcase Black lives from Black perspectives, without the need to add violence, sex, or musical numbers as a way of enticing audiences. Instead, it presents realistic, neighborhood, and family-specific tales that involved humans dealing with relatable quirks and tribulations of American life. The aforementioned *Good Times*, *The Jeffersons*, *A Different World*, *Insecure*, and countless other television shows and films over the past few decades are all descendants of *Five on the Black Hand Side*.

And if nothing else, its cast alone is a beautiful array of Black talent often undervalued when they appeared in predominately white media: Ja'net DuBois, who would star in *Good Times* and *I'm Gonna Git You Sucka* (1988); actor D'Urville Martin, who would write and direct one of the most iconic Blaxploitation films of all time, *Dolemite* (1975); future *Cosby Show* star Clarice Taylor; actor Glynn Turman, who would impress audiences two years later in *Cooley High* (1975); and Carl Franklin, director of *Devil in a Blue Dress* (1995). Everyone delivers stellar performances, particularly Jackson, whose strong theatrical cadence adds a hilarious exaggeration to the already over-the-top Mr. Brooks.

Five on the Black Hand Side is possibly the first film of its time to capture the inner machinations of the barbershop, a place where lively dialogue and interaction take place. Here, the shop is shown as the central hub for a basic all-boys club in which women aren't allowed and where a range of bolstering, honest, and not always agreeable conversation is had. A barber by trade, Mr. Brooks owns a local barbershop that becomes the second major set piece of the film outside the Brookses' apartment. In the barbershop, Mr. Brooks is much more aloof and relaxed, practically childish, cracking jokes with his coworkers, dishing out advice, and making his operation a chauvinistic "no women allowed" space, so much so that he requires a "treatment" of disinfection once a woman has entered. A fixture within the Black community, the barbershop would continue to be a staple in film and television after its appearance in *Five on the Black Hand Side*, like in Robert Townsend's

Hollywood Shuffle (1987), the hilariously iconic scene of Eddie Murphy's *Coming to America* (1988), *Barbershop* (2002), and its sequels and spinoffs, and HBO's *The Shop* series.

A Spotlight on ... Glynn Turman

Actor Glynn Turman (1947–) was the overlooked prince of Black cinema in the 1970s. Turman would make his strongest mark as Preach in 1975's *Cooley High*, though most will recognize him for his later work in post-1980s television, including *A Different World* and his fantastic turn in *Ma Rainey's Black Bottom* (2020). With a fifty-year career under his belt, credits as a director and producer, and work on the big and small screens, Turman's cinematic efforts have often been overlooked and underrated, but we can't ignore a solid decade of impressive, underplayed, and sometimes hilariously overacted but never boring performances, including in the Max Julien–produced and Gordon Parks Jr.–directed Western *Thomasine & Bushrod* (1974), *Together Brothers* (1974), *The River Niger* (1976), *A Hero Ain't Nothing but a Sandwich* (1977), and *Minstrel Man* (1977). He also manages to both dazzle and baffle in the 1976 Blaxploitation film *J.D.'s Revenge* and in *Penitentiary II* (1982).

BORN IN FLAMES

USA, 1983 • COLOR, 79 MINUTES

Honey (Honey), DJ from Radio Phoenix

DIRECTOR: Lizzie Borden **SCREENPLAY:** Lizzie Borden

STARRING: Honey (Honey), Adele Bertei (Isabel), Jean Satterfield
(Adelaide Norris), Florynce Kennedy (Zella Wylie),
Kathryn Bigelow (Newspaper Editor)

The political docufiction *Born in Flames* begins with a fake news report on the years following the Social Democratic War of Liberation, "the most peaceful revolution the world has ever known." What was supposed to have been a new era of prosperity, equality, and inclusion for modern society has apparently soured in recent times. Racism, sexism, and high levels of unemployment still run rampant in America. The response among groups of radical feminists living in New York City has been to organize gangs or armies across the city both as means of protection and social change. This dystopian vision is the framework for *Born in Flames*, which mixes contemporary social issues, post-punk, and science fiction into one of the most unique and revolutionary films in the history of independent cinema.

Born in Flames director Linda Elizabeth Borden was born in Detroit in the 1950s, adopting the first name Lizzie (after the notorious murder suspect) at a young age. After attending college at Wellesley, Borden moved to New York and became a writer for *Artforum* magazine before developing an interest in filmmaking and shooting her own movie, the experimental documentary *Regrouping* (1976). Borden began working on *Born in Flames* soon after, shooting when she

Honey gets an exclusive, on-the-street interview.

Zella (Florynce Kennedy) and Adelaide (Jean Satterfield) discuss political strategy.

could (and when she could afford to) over the course of several years. Influenced by Gillo Pontecorvo's legendary war film *The Battle of Algiers* (1966) and by her own experiences navigating the various, often fractured feminist organizations in the city, *Born in Flames* discussed women's issues across the intersection of race, class, and sexual orientation in a way that had not been approached before. Borden called on her own friends, artists she knew, and activists she worked with to appear in the film. Borden's ties to the downtown art scene, the blossoming No Wave movement,

and various feminist circles added to the film's authentic style. Direct action, armed revolution, the power of the press, and police brutality are a handful of many topics covered in the film.

Adelaide Norris, a college basketball player and part-time construction worker, is the founder of a feminist faction called the Women's Army, comprised mostly of Black women and lesbians. Two pirate radio stations are used to disseminate information, one headed by Isabel of Radio Ragazza and the other by Honey of Phoenix Radio. Meetings between the activists are intercut with scenes of women participating in various forms of political activism such as flyering, graffiti, and organized protests. The authorities, including two male federal agents, begin to form a dossier on the women, and view the army as vigilantes in need of arrest and punishment. A group of three white women editing a newspaper called *The Socialist Youth Review* believe the best tactic is to not disrupt the changes already made from the War of Liberation. Under the tutelage of an older feminist activist named Zella Wylie (played by the real-life lawyer and radical feminist activist Florynce Kennedy), Adelaide is more and more radicalized with each incident, eventually making the decision to bear arms and to travel to Africa to learn from women fighting in the Western Sahara. Upon her return to the United States, she is stopped by police and is eventually found dead under their custody—they claim by suicide—which finally ignites the splintered feminist organizations to band together.

Calling attention to the issues that still face the world today, *Born in Flames* feels as fresh and urgent as when it was released. Often mentioned is the pulsating soundtrack to the film, a sampling of popular soul, reggae, and underground post-punk anthems including the titular theme song, which is played in multiple sections of the film (it was written and performed by the legendary rock band the Red Crayola with X-Ray Spex member Lora Logic on lead vocals), and the punk-funk scorcher "Undercover Nation" by the Bloods, sung by Adele Bertei. Borden would next direct the independent film *Working Girls* (1986), an unflinchingly honest portrayal of the lives of

The legendary feminist actress Florynce Kennedy

sex workers inspired by some of the women she met while making *Born in Flames*, before having a series of disappointing creative experiences in Hollywood. Her first feature, however, has only grown in relevance since its release (it was restored in 2016 by Anthology Film Archives) and continues to be viewed and discussed by feminists and cinephiles alike.

Did You Know

One of the women who plays the three editors of *The Socialist Youth Review* is the Hollywood director Kathryn Bigelow, in one of her only known acting roles. Another is the Irish director Pat Murphy, whose film *Maeve* (1981) is often cited as Ireland's first feminist film. This was also the film debut of the actor Eric Bogosian, who plays a technician at the television station taken over by activists.

TWO-LANE BLACKTOP

USA, 1971 • COLOR, 102 MINUTES

The Girl (Laurie Bird) and The Driver (James Taylor)

DIRECTOR: Monte Hellman   **SCREENPLAY:** Rudy Wurlitzer, Will Corry

STARRING: James Taylor (The Driver), Dennis Wilson (The Mechanic),

Warren Oates (G.T.O.), Laurie Bird (The Girl)

Two-Lane Blacktop isn't just a movie. It's a state of mind. This cinematic mood piece isn't concerned with its barely existent plot or its characters, the hapless transparent drifters we watch cross America. Instead, the focus and the allure of this strange, almost dreamlike cruise is the oddly peaceful ride we aimlessly take with no destination in sight. When this movie was made, Charles Manson and his murderous family had just shaken up America, particularly the L.A. countercul- ture scene, from which folk singer James Taylor and Beach Boys drummer Dennis Wil- son emerged. The Laurel Canyon duo found themselves the unlikely stars of this picture by sheer coincidence, and yet their respective on-screen debuts feel kismet in this story fol- lowing two drifters on a cross-country journey to nowhere, racing random strangers along the way for quick cash to keep driving onward.

Taylor, whose light, honey-sweet voice serenaded listeners over the airwaves, was dealing with alcoholism and depression at the time while Wilson was battling similar demons after being closely involved with the Manson Family a couple of years before the film's production. The darkness in both men's lives seems to work well in bringing their stoic, detached characters to life in the bare-bones, empty world they drift in and out of. On their journey, the duo meets a wandering hippie girl (Laurie Bird) and an antagonist kindred spirit (Warren Oates), and by proxy, the audience is introduced to a slew of hitchhiking strangers with their own agendas, baggage, and journeys in the short time we know them. It's an ensemble piece with little emphasis on the ensemble, instead highlighting a revolving door of characters, all harboring their own neuroses and a com- mon fascination with cars.

Two-Lane Blacktop is dry and monotonous, but there's a rhythmic life in the editing and within Monte Hellman's camerawork that is vibrant and haunting. It also brought a new life and appreciation for car culture to the screen. While cars had already seen a surge of popularity in cinema, a sporty vehicle was merely an added bonus in most of the films. *Bullitt*'s (1968) wild chase scene may be the film's most memorable aspect, but it's a cop drama first. Herbie the Love Bug is known for its adorable shenanigans and comedic moments rather than what's under its hood in *The Love Bug* (1968). But *Two-Lane Blacktop* is

Beach Boys drummer Dennis Wilson in his first and only film

all about the automobiles, so much so that viewers understand more about the cars than the characters themselves. Our leads travel on the iconic Route 66 highway in a souped-up, defunct 1955 Chevrolet 150, stopping frequently to make sure the car is in tip-top shape and pushing the speed limit to embrace the power of its engine. Like New Zealand's *Vanishing Point*, released in the same year, *Two-Lane Blacktop* captured the cultural zeitgeist of 1971 through car culture. For America that meant a dark, lonely landscape, as the future felt uncertain and dismal with the hippie era waning, giving rise to a more somber reality.

Two-Lane Blacktop found critical appreciation at the time of its release but was a box-office failure. It marked the first and last time both Taylor and Wilson would act in dramatic film roles and it also captured the Route 66 highway system, a paved transient road that served as the primary route for going West. Winding from Illinois to California, the highway was used heavily for nearly sixty years before being dismantled and replaced by the interstate highway system. The long driving scenes on Route 66 give *Two-Lane Blacktop* its feeling of a film lost in thought. Despite its trudging nature, the one-of-a-kind drama maintains its intrigue through perfectly blocked scenes and a script that has the right amount of exposition to tell us everything we need to know about these two men that they refuse to say aloud to anyone else about their loneliness and social apathy. It's not a perfect film, but, like the rhythmic roll of wheels on pavement, it will pull you into its tranquil pacing from the first scene.

Genre-ly Speaking

There's something appealing about hitting the highway and going nowhere in particular while experiencing existential quandaries about life. *Bullitt* (1968) and *Vanishing Point* (1971) brought excitement and thrill to the cinematic car chase, while *Easy Rider* (1969) and *Two-Lane Blacktop* highlighted the pensive loneliness of a drifter's life on the road. The two similar but very different genres of road movies have their share of contenders. For more of the drifter on the road, see *Wanda* (1970), *Badlands* (1973), *Paris, Texas* (1984), *My Own Private Idaho* (1991), *On the Road* (2012), and *American Honey* (2016).

Warren Oates stars alongside newcomers Dennis Wilson and James Taylor.

EMMA MAE
(A.K.A. BLACK SISTER'S REVENGE)

USA, 1976 • COLOR, 100 MINUTES

Emma Mae (Jerri Hayes) and her cousins enjoy the sun.

DIRECTOR: Jamaa Fanaka   **SCREENPLAY:** Jamaa Fanaka

STARRING: Jerri Hayes (Emma Mae), Ernest Williams II (Jesse Amos),

Charles D. Brooks III (Ezekiel "Zeke" Johnson), Leopoldo Mandeville (Chay),

Malik Carter ("Big Daddy" Johnson), Eddie Allen (James), Gammy Burdett (Daisy

Stansell), Teri Taylor (Dara Stansell), Synthia Saint James (Ulika Stansell)

uring the production of *Emma Mae*, mainstream Hollywood was in the process of seizing on low-budget films set in urban environments centered around Black leads dealing in crime, karate, and drugs. These films were exploding at the box office as the crumbling studio system was looking for a lifeline after their glitzy, big-budget pictures, often out of touch with the changing times, began consistently bombing. In turn, studio execs began to take a keen interest in the African American market for the first time in Hollywood history. The common denominator became clear: Black urban audiences were seeing Black-led movies, causing a boom in the production of these films, leading to an exploitation of circumstances that has led to the now commonplace term for this movement, Blaxploitation.

But while Blaxploitation was taking theaters across the country by storm, a different genre of films began to blossom from young Black film students attending UCLA. The prestigious film school had its first Black graduate in 1953; Ike Jones would go on to produce the severely under seen and underappreciated Sammy Davis Jr. drama *A Man Called Adam* (1966). Afterward, a bevy of cinephiles flocked to the UCLA film school when its chair increased funding to register more students of color. During the late 1960s into the early 1990s, this new class of students worked to depict alternative stories about Black life that didn't focus on crime, drugs, and the ghetto and that moved away from conventional subjects and methods of storytelling. This booming era of cinematic output has become known as the L.A. Rebellion, signifying a shift

in filmmaking standards and desires coming from the West Coast. This wave gave rise to a number of influential, outstanding directors, including Julie Dash, Charles Burnett, Haile Gerima, and *Emma Mae* director Jamaa Fanaka.

Fanaka's *Emma Mae* is the first independent film released to be associated with the movement, and, although it is a prototype of its genre, it still manages to be a type of hybrid film that isn't often made today. It's part fish-out-of-water story, part coming of age, part family drama, and part revolutionary tale of Black female empowerment. In it, we meet Emma Mae, a country girl from

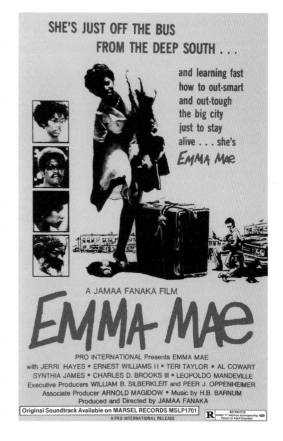

SHE'S JUST OFF THE BUS
FROM THE DEEP SOUTH . . .

and learning fast
how to out-smart
and out-tough
the big city
just to stay
alive . . . she's
EMMA MAE

A JAMAA FANAKA FILM

EMMA MAE

PRO INTERNATIONAL Presents EMMA MAE
with JERRI HAYES • ERNEST WILLIAMS II • TERI TAYLOR • AL COWART
SYNTHIA JAMES • CHARLES D. BROOKS III • LEOPOLDO MANDEVILLE
Executive Producers WILLIAM B. SILBERKLEIT and PEER J. OPPENHEIMER
Associate Producer ARNOLD MAGIDOW • Music by H.B. BARNUM
Produced and Directed by JAMAA FANAKA
Original Soundtrack Available on MARSEL RECORDS MSLP1701 ☐ R RESTRICTED
Under 17 requires accompanying
Parent or Adult Guardian
A PRO INTERNATIONAL RELEASE

Emma Mae knows something's not right.

Mississippi sent to live with her cousins in the big city of Compton. When she steps off the bus in her humble and threadbare clothes, Emma is immediately met with hostility and judgment from her own family. Her challenge is to navigate this new environment that is as foreign to her as she is to it. Emma is resilient though and soon finds social acceptance, love, and heartbreak, and when the time comes, she kicks ass. She endures it all with an unbreakable spirit, a natural charm, and a deep kindness that transcends the confines of the screen.

It's a true shame that actress Jerri Hayes never went on to star in other films, as she gives a gregariously delightful performance as Emma. Hayes captures and effectively transmits the sweet naiveté of the character, and Fanaka and his camera seem to adore her and know exactly how to make her shine. Hayes's charm dazzles in all its forms: every kind word out of her mouth and gesture feels sincere, but when she needs to put the heat on someone to show she's not a fool, we feel the burning rays of its emission. Hayes's sensitive and passionate performance and Fanaka's script blend effortlessly together to bring Emma into a fully realized character. In the film's climax, Emma is betrayed by someone close to her. When she confronts the culprit, Hayes perfectly expresses Emma's sadness, resolve, and subsequent rage, giving balance to the sweet, tender character we've known throughout the film and showing us a dynamic woman ready to explode.

A detailed description of *Emma Mae*'s plot couldn't do this humorous, exciting story justice. It's a film that just is. It's a happening—a place to be. It's Compton L.A. in the 1970s experienced by Black teenagers in all of its wild, silly, and outrageous glory. *Emma Mae*'s closest counterpart would come a year later with Michael Schultz's fantastically endearing and tragic *Cooley High*. But where *Cooley High* fits the mold of stories highlighting male sexuality and aggressive behavior, *Emma Mae* is a rarity in its tender geniality and its focus on a Black woman coming of age.

This under seen and underappreciated gem is often miscategorized and lumped into the Blaxploitation genre, which is a disservice to the story put forth by Fanaka. It's no surprise that distributors attempted to drum up intrigue for the film when marketing its video release years later. It was given the title *Black Sister's Revenge* with the poster art portraying a trio of barely clothed women and one with a gun. This misrepresentation is likely the explanation for the general lack of awareness surrounding the film. It's a lighthearted drama showcasing a young woman experiencing love and heartbreak and developing self-assuredness in the process. It's also a film grounded in a keen sense of place—the post-1965 Watts uprising, depicted in scenes of police brutality. But Fanaka manages to express the reality while not exploiting it. Emma's fight isn't against the Man, it's against the expectations

and callousness of others. It's a charming film starring an even more magnetic lead with a superb cast of actors who all feel natural and united in their desire to make a good film. Everyone involved succeeded with flying colors, which makes *Emma Mae* a truly special film.

Genre-ly Speaking

Though it's not a genre of film, the L.A. Rebellion covers a finite set of films made in a designated era between 1967 and ending in or around 2000. These films often share themes of life in its various forms experienced by members of the African diaspora. All these films were made by members of the UCLA film department who attended the school from the 1960s through the 1980s, and many continued to make films after they graduated from one of most influential graduate classes of the twentieth century. Larry Clark—*Passing Through* (1977); Charles Burnett—*Killer of Sheep* (1978); Haile Gerima—*Bush Mama* (1979), *Ashes and Embers* (1982), and *Sanfoka* (1993); Jamaa Fanaka—*Penitentiary* (1979); Julie Dash—*Illusions* (1982) and *Daughters of the Dust* (1991); Billy Woodberry—*Bless Their Little Hearts* (1984); Zeinabu irene Davis—*Compensation* (1999).

LADIES AND GENTLEMEN, THE FABULOUS STAINS

USA, 1982 • COLOR, 87 MINUTES

Marin Kanter, Diane Lane, and Laura Dern onstage as the Stains

DIRECTOR: Lou Adler   **SCREENPLAY:** Nancy Dowd (credited to Rob Morton)
STARRING: Diane Lane (Corinne Burns), Laura Dern (Jessica McNeil), Marin Kanter (Tracy Burns), Ray Winstone (Billy), Peter Donat (Harley Dennis)

Punk rock was in full swing by the early 1980s and had already crossed into the film world several times, in both documentary (*The Blank Generation*, *Urgh! A Music War*, *The Decline of Western Civilization*) and narrative film (*Jubilee*, *Rock 'n' Roll High School*, *Times Square*). Lou Adler, an icon of '60s music who developed several famous artists such as the Mamas and the Papas and Carole King, had branched out into film by this time, producing several music-related movies, both documentary (*Monterey Pop*) and narrative (*The Rocky Horror Picture Show*). He even sat in the director's chair at least once, most notably for the Cheech and Chong classic *Up in Smoke*.

In the late 1970s he was brought a script from the screenwriter Nancy Dowd, who had penned the Paul Newman hockey classic *Slapshot* and become an Oscar winner for *Coming Home*. Dowd had recently seen the legendary punk band the Ramones in concert and was interested in writing a movie about female punks. Women musicians have always struggled in the music industry compared to their male counterparts, and a nuanced story of teen girls in the punk scene seemed like a fresh, welcome idea. The story centers on Corinne, a seventeen-year-old desperate to leave her uninspiring and economically barren hometown. After the death of her mother, Corinne forms a punk band with her sister and cousin and they go on tour. Dowd brought in Caroline Coon, a writer for the music magazine *Melody Maker* and one-time manager for the Clash, as a consultant to lend an authentic voice to the film. Several real-life musicians were also cast, such as Steve Jones and Paul Cook from the Sex Pistols, Paul Simonon of the Clash, Fee Waybill and Vince Welnick of the Tubes, and the L.A. avant-garde smut band Black Randy and the Metrosquad. Alongside these actual, working punk musicians were the three actresses who played the Stains, all of whom were actresses in their teens. Diane Lane, as lead singer Corinne "Third Degree" Burns, was fourteen years old when filming began in 1980 and had only appeared in one movie prior to *The Fabulous Stains*. Laura Dern was also in her early teens when she signed up to play fellow Stains bandmate (and cousin to the Burns girls), Jessica McNeil. Marin Kanter, the oldest of the three (but not by much), made her film debut playing Corinne's sister Diane, guitarist for the Stains.

The film opens with a news reporter (played by Peter Donat) interviewing Corinne, who has just been fired from her fast-food

Diane Lane as Corrine "Third Degree" Burns

The Stains (and their Skunks)

job while the cameras are rolling. The news segment begins as a story about the town Corinne lives in (Charlestown, Pennsylvania) but quickly becomes about Corinne herself: an agitated, disaffected young person in a town with little opportunity or inspiration. When the reporter pays her a follow-up visit, he finds Corinne even more aloof and avoidant than before her mother died; she lights up a cigarette and begins painting her eyelids with a bright eye pencil as the reporter comments, "You're unemployed, broke, and cynical!" Corinne's only response is to introduce the rest of the Stains, who share the same blank stares. We eventually meet Jessica's mother (and aunt to Corinne and Diane), Linda (played by Christine Lahti), and it's clear that she has little control over these girls and their disillusionment with life.

Corinne attends a concert featuring the Looters, an opening young punk band from the UK, and a headlining band called the Metal Corpses, a holdback from the prog rock/glam era still trying to cash in on their former glory.

The two groups are generationally out of sync and butt heads often, and in an effort to defuse the situation, tour manager Lawnboy (played by Barry Ford, formerly of the reggae band Merger) decides to hire the Stains to be the third act on the tour, despite having never seen them play. It's true the Stains have no musical experience, but Corinne soon realizes that creating a look and persona, which includes dying her hair in a black-and-white pattern, donning a sexy outfit including a see-through red blouse, and creating an extreme makeup look reminiscent of Siouxsie Sioux or Divine, can be just as effective. Despite the theatrics, the Stains find touring life to be unglamorous and at times dangerous. Early on in the tour they discover that one of the Metal Corpses has overdosed in a bathroom at the venue they're about to perform in and the girls are visibly shaken. It's a harsh reminder of just how young and green the Stains truly are among the much older men on the road.

Corinne's provocation continues and soon also includes several passionate onstage speeches, including the phrase "we don't put out," meant to be both semi-literal and a clarion call for women's independence and self-reliance. The band catches the attention of a female journalist and they gain a steady following of young female fans who echo the same "fuck you" attitude as Corinne, in the same bold makeup and skimpy clothing that the band wears. The throngs of young girls now brazenly running around town—who have begun to call themselves the Skunks based on the black-and-white hair of their favorite band—are a powerful sight and remind us of what would later be called the riot grrrl movement almost twenty years later. Meanwhile, the much-older male musicians on the tour, especially Looters lead singer Billy (played by British character actor Ray Winstone) grow increasingly annoyed with the sudden reception the Stains are getting. Despite Billy and Corinne's brief romantic fling while on the road, the two bands eventually clash, and soon Billy begins his own tirade about authenticity and selling out that eventually makes the Skunks turn on Corinne and the band.

Nancy Dowd and Lou Adler also reportedly clashed over the ending of the film; Dowd wanted the ending to feature the band touring in Europe and Adler wanted the band to be famous. After the fighting and Dowd's claim that she had been sexually harassed on set by a crewmember, she left the film and had her name removed (the official screenwriter of the film is listed under a fake name, Rob Morton). The movie sat untouched for two entire years until Adler decided to finally give it his ending, showing a much more polished version of the Stains, now on television, enjoying

a taste of commercial success. It was eventually shelved after it failed at the box office, but became a cult favorite many years later, due mostly to cable television (appearing on the series *Night Flight*) and repertory screenings. Unsurprisingly, the movie was name-dropped several times by female artists and musicians in the 1990s as a source of inspiration for the riot grrrl movement. The lasting power of *Ladies and Gentlemen, the Fabulous Stains* may be the idea that these young girls are not in a safe, cute world, and that being just as gritty and unscrupulous as the boys was the only avenue to fulfill their punk rock dream.

Cult Connections

In 1999, director Sarah Jacobson (of *Mary Jane's Not a Virgin Anymore* fame) and filmmaker Sam Green directed a twelve-minute documentary short entitled *The Fabulous Stains: Behind the Movie*, which was originally pitched as a piece for *Split Screen*, a television show about independent film hosted by filmmaker John Pierson. It includes exclusive behind-the-scenes photographs and interviews with screenwriter Nancy Dowd, director Lou Adler, actresses Diane Lane, Christine Lahti, and Debbie Rochon, and musicians Fee Waybill, Steve Jones, and Paul Cook. In the short, Dowd explains her subsequent departure from the film, as well as her reaction seeing the movie on late-night television after many years.

LITTLE DARLINGS

USA, 1980 • COLOR, 96 MINUTES

The lead darlings Tatum O'Neal and Kristy McNichol

DIRECTOR: Ron Maxwell   **SCREENPLAY:** Kimi Peck, Dalene Young
STARRING: Tatum O'Neal (Ferris), Kristy McNichol (Angel), Armand
Assante (Gary), Matt Dillon (Randy), Margaret Blye (Ms. Bright), Nicolas
Coster (Mr. Whitney), Krista Errickson (Cinder), Alexa Kenin (Dana),
Abby Bluestone (Chubby), Cynthia Nixon (Sunshine)

Teenage sexuality wasn't a new topic by the time *Little Darlings* was released at the onset of the 1980s, but it certainly hadn't been handled as openly and honestly before. Classic Hollywood delicately touched on the topic in the 1950s as the concept of the teenager came into its own in postwar America. *Tea and Sympathy* (1956), *Blue Denim* (1959), *A Summer Place* (1959), and *Splendor in the Grass* (1961) were brave enough to handle coming-of-age and the pressures of sex as their focus, but with kid gloves as the Production Code still prevented much nuance or realism. Premarital sex in this era was so taboo that the teens in such films endured the breakdown of their families, their mental health, or negative effects on those around them.

By 1980, teenagers coming of age and having sex wasn't a scary afterschool-special tragedy anymore. In fact, sex is apparently so commonplace among a group of teenage girls at summer camp in *Little Darlings* that they've all convinced themselves that everyone has done it. So, when a crude joke in the bathroom reveals that there are two virgins in the camp—Angel, a lower-class, hard-nosed teen struggling with intimacy issues, and Ferris, a wealthy girl often ostracized because of her status and dealing with her parents' divorce—this revelation turns into a summer-long bet that divides the campers over who will lose her virginity first. Throughout the season, the two girls debate love and sex, expressing their personal beliefs of what it should be and generally wondering what the big deal is, while Ferris falls in love with the camp counselor and Angel's attention is laser-focused on Randy, a dreamy fox attending the all-boys camp across the lake.

One of the first films to focus solely on teenage girls' lust and the chase to get laid, *Little Darlings*'s edginess is a primary reason its legacy as a cult classic has remained. Our incredibly young heroines break into bathrooms for condoms and eagerly pursue all the details about who's getting laid and how. Though largely forgotten, the film is a precursor to the male-dominated sex-comedy genre that would gain traction a year later with the arrival of *Porky's*. Movies centered on the male quest to have sex or lose one's virginity became run-of-the-mill after the 1980s and well into the early 2000s, almost defining comedy in the latter era. *Little Darlings* contemporaneously got roped in with those types of films, leaving it overlooked by audiences today, even

Matt Dillon as Randy

Kristy McNichol as Angel

though young women are hard-pressed to see their emotional struggles with sex presented on-screen before the likes of *Eighth Grade* or *Booksmart*, made decades later.

Little Darlings captures the essence of its era, bringing forth an intense nostalgia when watched today, whether for sun-drenched summer days of youth or the dizziness of being young and in love for the first time. These moments of memory are captured by director of photography Bedrich Batka's hazy, golden-hued outdoor shots that highlight the vibrant natural settings, while Kimi Peck and Dalene Young's screenplay is energized with an exceptional soundtrack that includes tracks by Blondie and the Cars. Despite some of the coarse language and subject matter, there's a genuine tenderness present throughout the movie, a gentle juxtaposition of the girls being girls and behaving

in ways usually attributed to boys. They fight hard and smoke cigarettes (good luck keeping track of how many cigarettes Angel lights up), they're obsessed with sex, and there's a massive food fight scene. They also pick flowers, play flutes, and lazily read books to pass the time, moments that aren't present in films like *Animal House* and *Porky's*. *Little Darlings* exhibits an array of intellectually stimulated pubescent girls and they're complex.

Tatum O'Neal and Kristy McNichol are fantastic leads; both of their characters grow more sensitive and lovable throughout the film. McNichol especially shines, delivering a sympathetic performance that subtly reveals confusion and apprehension beneath a layer of self-assurance, particularly in her scenes with Matt Dillon. Here is when her bad-girl façade cracks as she gets closer to doing the deed. During a climactic moment together with Randy, Angel stumbles, struggling to get her feelings under control as she searches for excuses to not lose her virginity. Everyone has told her this is not a big deal, but she suddenly realizes it is, in fact, a very big deal to her. Dillon and McNichol have strong chemistry, playing well off each other by being alternatively sweet and rancid, revealing their characters' pain, sadness, and comfort with each other.

McNichol went on to have a rocky career in film and television before quitting the business in the mid-1990s. Having shot to stardom as a child actor in the 1970s, McNichol admitted to having a nervous breakdown two years after *Little Darlings*. Later, she came out as a lesbian, and one can't help but detect a lesbian subtext in *Little Darlings*, as Angel is not initially interested in boys or the thought of having sex with them. It's only when she is pressured to fit in that Randy becomes the object of her desire. She's then confronted with dissatisfied feelings that she can't explain when alone with Randy. These moments may not be overt but are notable considering *Little Darlings* has a large lesbian fan base.

O'Neal was also a 1970s screen legend and had become the youngest person ever to win a competitive Oscar at age ten for her role in *Paper Moon* (1973), which she starred in alongside her father, Ryan O'Neal. However, both girls lack any baggage of Hollywood royalty or clout here. They authentically appear to be two teenage girls figuring their way through life among their peers and trying to fit in. Both do stellar jobs among an ensemble cast that includes a young Cynthia Nixon of later *Sex and the City* fame. *Little Darlings* was a minor success upon its release, but it

reached cult status thanks to television airings in the 1980s and '90s that gave it a wider exposure among a new audience. Nevertheless, the film has some music rights issues, requiring heavy edits on TV broadcasts and preventing a DVD release, making it one of the film anomalies that hasn't yet made it into the post-VHS world. We hope this entry introduces *Little Darlings* to a wider audience looking for an atypical, all-girls sex comedy.

Cult Connections

Along with O'Neal and McNichol, Brooke Shields and Jodie Foster were the go-to teenage actresses at the time known for their talent and ability to undertake mature roles. Foster, O'Neal, and McNichol had all been involved in *The Bad News Bears* (1976) during its production a few years earlier, with McNichol having been cast but replaced by O'Neal and Foster having auditioned for the lead part. O'Neal had always been the first choice for *Little Darlings*' Ferris, but Foster, who had just starred in *Freaky Friday* (1976), had been considered for the role of Angel Bright. She instead made her final teenage-era film in another TCM Underground feature, *Foxes* (1980), for which McNichol had incidentally auditioned. An offer for the role had also gone to Shields, who instead made the controversial *Blue Lagoon* released the same year, a film that McNichol had been considered for.

MARY JANE'S NOT A VIRGIN ANYMORE

USA, 1996 • COLOR AND B&W, 98 MINUTES

Jane (Lisa Gerstein) and Tom (Chris Enright) get cozy.

DIRECTOR: Sarah Jacobson   **SCREENPLAY:** Sarah Jacobson

STARRING: Lisa Gerstein (Jane), Chris Enright (Tom), Greg Cruikshank (Dave), Beth Allen (Ericka), Marny Snyder Spoons (Grace)

The female coming-of-age film suddenly got a punk rock kick in the pants when the feminist filmmaker Sarah Jacobson released *Mary Jane's Not a Virgin Anymore*, a story of a recent high school graduate navigating her love life among the various employees of an art-house movie theater in the Minneapolis–Saint Paul area. Prior to *Mary Jane*, few, if any, films depicted honest, frank conversations about female sexuality, let alone scenes where young women were experiencing both the thrills and discomforts of sexual discovery.

Born in 1971, Jacobson had grown up watching the teen sex comedies of the 1980s and felt their focus was always on the guys, never the girls. After attending film school at the San Francisco Art Institute under the tutelage of the professor and beloved underground filmmaker George Kuchar, Jacobson began making her own short films, including the twenty-five-minute, black-and-white radical revenge film *I Was a Teenage Serial Killer* about a woman who takes matters into her own hands after a lifetime of male mistreatment. Jacobson allegedly wrote, directed, and shot the film for about $1,600 and also distributed the short entirely on her own. It became an underground cult hit and would allow Jacobson to begin work on her first (and only) feature.

Mary Jane's Not a Virgin Anymore is the story of Jane, a suburban high school senior who spends her free time working at the big-city movie theater with a mixed group of alternative twenty-somethings. Right off the bat, she unremarkably loses her virginity to Steve on a blanket in a graveyard. Disillusioned by the experience, she swears off sex and begins hearing the terrible stories of her coworkers and their first times, which makes her feel only slightly better. Jane has a close connection to the gay manager of the movie theater, Dave, who is her confidant and also cool and citywise (she wishes she were both). She also has supportive friendships with coworkers Ericka and Grace, both of whom have moved in and out of romances and sexual encounters over the years with many of the straight male employees. Jane develops a crush on Ryan, the sweet nerd of the group, even though the dreamy Tom seems to be taking an interest in her. Drama ensues, and Jane eventually discovers her own sexual power, both solo and with a positive sexual experience with Tom. Once she realizes that intimacy has everything to do with her own wants and desires and not just those of her partner, Jane moves on from the theater, older and wiser than she was before.

Produced over the course of several years and released in 1996, *Mary Jane* is a bold, unapologetic look at the sexual life of a young woman. Its focus on female pleasure and the often-disappointing experience of teenage dating is shown with humor and humility. Conversational and buoyant, *Mary Jane* could easily rub shoulders with the '90s music-meets-hangout-style films of Richard Linklater, Kevin Smith, and Gregg Araki. More importantly, though, the film sat at a crossroads of the era's alternative/feminist/punk rock subculture, which included the riot grrrl scene, the D.I.Y. ethos of art and culture, and the crucial, pre-internet community of fanzine creators and underground press. By referencing these trends, Jacobson's

Sarah Jacobson, the film's writer/director

comedy-drama situated itself within the deep culture of indie/art-house films and theaters that were prevalent at the time. To that end, *Mary Jane* is a brilliant time capsule of a specific time and place. At a moment when a proliferation of female art exploded across many different disciplines, Jacobson cast women musicians in her film (including two members of the punk band the Loudmouths) and used several female-fronted bands on the soundtrack, like Babes in Toyland, Red Aunts, and Tiger Trap. Jacobson also garnered financial support for *Mary Jane* from the director Tamra Davis and received accolades for the film from both Kim Gordon of Sonic Youth and the director Allison Anders.

The film premiered at the Chicago Underground Film Festival in August 1996 and quickly sold out its screenings at Sundance and South by Southwest the year after. Jacobson tragically died young at the age of thirty-two from endometrial cancer but undoubtedly left a powerful legacy and body of work to inspire the next generation of underground feminist filmmakers.

Cult Connections

There are several cameos in *Mary Jane's Not a Virgin Anymore*, including Jacobson's former professor and mentor, George Kuchar, AFI lead singer Davey Havok, and Dead Kennedys frontman Jello Biafra, who assumes multiple roles as complaint-filled patrons of the movie theater.

Did You Know

Having already created a powerful body of work at such a young age, one can only wonder what the director Sarah Jacobson could have accomplished, especially in the current push for inclusion and better opportunities for women in film. Jacobson was only thirty-two years old when she passed away from endometrial cancer, and with her a giant hole was left in the indie filmmaking community and among grrrl powered film fans everywhere. In addition to the short and feature films she released during her life, Jacobson also directed music videos for the bands Fluffy and Man . . . or Astro-man?, and wrote for an assortment of national music and film press including Punk Planet and Indiewire.

After her passing in 2004, the director's family and friends created the Sarah Jacobson Film Grant, which awards yearly funds to self-identifying women and gender nonconforming creators who share Jacobson's ethos of socially relevant, do-it-yourself filmmaking. Past winners have included a diverse roster of directors including Marie Losier for the music documentary *The Ballad of Genesis and Lady Jaye* and Angelo Madsen Minax for his essay film, *North by Current*.

Additionally, since 2005, Jacobson's papers have been included at the Fales Library and Special Collections at New York University. The archive includes production materials from her various film and writing projects, artifacts from her activism work, and an assortment of audio cassettes, videos, flyers, and fanzines collected from Jacobson's life.

ROLLER BOOGIE

USA, 1979 • COLOR, 104 MINUTES

Stars of the roller disco, Terry (Linda Blair) and Bobby (Jim Bray)

DIRECTOR: Mark L. Lester   **SCREENPLAY:** Barry Schneider, Irwin Yablans (story)
STARRING: Linda Blair (Terry Barkley), Jim Bray (Bobby James), Beverly Garland
(Lillian Barkley), Roger Perry (Roger Barkley), James Van Patten (Hoppy)

The movies have always been attentive when it comes to cultural fads, and lucky for us, they were front and center during the memorable but short-lived roller disco trend of the late '70s. Producer Irwin Yablans, right off the success of John Carpenter's *Halloween* in 1978, wanted a topical teen film for his new company, Compass International Pictures. Actress Linda Blair had appeared in several made-for-television movies following the worldwide success of *The Exorcist* in 1973 (she also made a brief return to the character of Regan MacNeil in the ill-received *Exorcist II: The Heretic* in 1977). She was looking to expand her resume beyond horror by the time the script for *Roller Boogie* came around. When he was hired to direct the film, Mark L. Lester already had a handful of entertaining action and drive-in flicks under his belt, including the Claudia Jennings eighteen-wheeler classic *Truck Stop Women* (1974) and the stuntmen-centered crime film *Stunts* (1977) starring Robert Forster. *Roller Boogie* seemed like the kind of fun he was known for.

To play the romantic male lead, producers turned to a young, artistic, competitive roller skater named Jim Bray, initially cast only as a skate double. He had never acted before (or since) and was actually forced to give up his amateur status to take the part. In the film, he plays Bobby James, a Venice Beach, California, skater and roller rink employee with dreams to go professional one day. He's pretty much front and center in the big opening scene of the movie, which consists of a splashy group skate number where muscular, tanned bodies are rolling to, appropriately enough, Cher's

"Hell on Wheels." As one can imagine, the fashions are one of the most memorable aspects of the film, a time capsule of the tight and barely there. At one point, the group whizzes by a couple who are, confoundingly, making out on top of a dumpster. Amidst the hot pants and high-cut bathing suits, one thing is for certain: Venice is absolutely roller skate crazy, and Bobby is their king.

Enter Terry Barkley (Blair), a wealthy girl from Beverly Hills whose destiny is to become a Julliard-trained classical flautist. Her parents (played by Beverly Garland and Roger Perry) are too concerned with their lavish lifestyles to pay attention to what she's doing, including when she goes down to the beach to skate. When Terry and her friend Lana (played by Kimberly Beck) show up on the

Terry gets ready to hit the boardwalk.

boardwalk, Terry is immediately impressed with Bobby's skills. He tries to engage her, but she plays hard to get. Everybody eventually ends up at Jammers, the hottest skating rink in town. The place is owned by an older man (named, yes, Jammer), a former roller derby competitor and Bobby's boss. It's here that the next big roller-skating montage happens, a dynamic sequence in which beautiful people roll across the screen in satin disco outfits as "Boogie Wonderland" by Earth, Wind, and Fire blasts from the speakers.

Many of the extras in these scenes were professional roller skaters (and, appropriately enough, many of them appeared in *Xanadu* a

FROM TOP: Bobby shows off in front of Terry and friends. • Terry and Bobby at the big roller-skating contest

year later). Bobby and Terry finally connect via a very flirty conversation, and she asks him to give her lessons for the big roller boogie contest Jammers is hosting. Bobby is willing, despite her lack of seriousness in both skating and dating, and his friends aren't much help either, teasing him for thinking he can score a rich girl. Meanwhile, Terry's home life is a world away from the raucousness of the boardwalk. Days are spent by the pool with Lana and their annoying preppy friend, Franklin (Christopher S. Nelson), discussing their almost complete abandonment by their busy, rich parents. At one point, Terry's mother does come home, and Terry confesses that she doesn't want to spend her days being their little flute prodigy anymore. Her mother offers her a plethora of prescription drugs from her designer purse, but Terry isn't interested; she simply wants to win a roller boogie contest at the beach.

Terry eventually runs away from home and goes directly to Bobby as a group of commercial real estate thugs visit Jammer and blackmail him at gunpoint to sell them the roller-skating rink. Bobby, Terry, and Bobby's friend Phones (so named because he wears giant headphones connected to a cassette player strapped across his chest every single day) witness the interaction and sense something is wrong, and their instincts are correct: Jammers is being sold and there will be no roller boogie contest after all. Naturally, the kids band together to attempt to save Jammers from the thugs, but will they do it in time before the big contest? Will Terry's parents eventually see her passion for the roller disco isn't just a phase? Will the Venice Beach boardwalk live to see another choreographed skating sequence?

Roller Boogie is a perfect representation of the high-watt glamour of our brief roller skate obsession. It was essentially the last teen movie stop for Linda Blair before she did a slew of B-movie horror and cult films starting in the early 1980s. Impressively, she did a lot of her own skating in the film despite having a double for some of the trickier scenes. Despite negative critical reviews, *Roller Boogie* did fairly well at the box office and Jim Bray became a bona fide teen star, despite never appearing in another movie again. This one-of-a-kind extravaganza has since become a beloved cult classic, especially as a memento of late-1970s Los Angeles and the world's brief fascination with disco and roller-skating.

Genre-ly Speaking

Roller Boogie was one of several films made in the 1970s and early 1980s centered around roller-skating. If you feel like diving back into a world on wheels, check out:

Kansas City Bomber (1972)

Unholy Rollers (1972)

Rollerball (1975)

Skatetown U.S.A. (1979)

Xanadu (1980)

Get Rollin' (1980)

THE DECLINE OF WESTERN CIVILIZATION

USA, 1981 • COLOR AND B&W, 100 MINUTES

A punk rock fan discussing the music

DIRECTOR: Penelope Spheeris
STARRING: Alice Bag Band, Black Flag, Circle Jerks, Fear, The Germs, X

irector Penelope Spheeris waited tables to put herself through film school and began her career working with comedian Albert Brooks, making short movies for the first season of *Saturday Night Live*. In 1981, she made her first feature-length film, a documentary about the punk rock scene in Los Angeles called *The Decline of Western Civilization*. Punk had largely been ignored by the mainstream American press, and the film marked one of the first attempts to capture the high-energy, antiestablishment movement. Interspersed with musical performances by several seminal L.A. punk bands such as Black Flag, the Germs, the Alice Bag Band, X, and the Circle Jerks are interviews with the band members, frequently in their own homes. Musicians were not the only people featured in the film; others who contributed regularly to the scene—club owners,

managers, fanzine writers, and fans—were also allowed to express their thoughts. Perhaps the most fascinating technique used in the documentary is Spheeris's up-close-and-personal interview style, which includes spontaneously lobbing questions at her subjects on camera. She takes some of the punks to task on the bigger questions, ones that mainstream media outlets often overlook, such as how they live and how much money they make from their music. The filmmaker's frankness is on full display in her interview with Darby Crash, lead singer of the Germs. Known for his outrageous stage antics and his guttural punk howls, he is asked what kind of drugs he takes onstage and why, while he casually cooks breakfast in his kitchen. It proves to be an ominous conversation, as the documentary was likely the last footage shot of Crash before his suicide-by-overdose in 1980.

The legendary Alice Bag onstage

A young punk interviewee **OPPOSITE FROM TOP:** Exene Cervenka and John Doe of X •
Punk fans attending a concert

Edgy and exciting moments fill the documentary. Scenes with the band X show guitar player and co-lead singer John Doe (who would later act in several independent and Hollywood films) giving someone a homemade tattoo. During the Circle Jerks performance, their mosh pit escalates into an actual fight, and the mayhem is followed by a series of black-and-white interviews with punk fans and musicians discussing their lifestyles. Many of them are alienated, hateful of authority, and willing to incite or participate in violence.

Later, bands like the Alice Bag Band—one of the few punk bands on the scene fronted by a woman of color—perform alongside the band Fear, who begins to antagonize the crowd and exchange spit with members of the audience. A man from the front row storms the stage and starts a fight with the lead singer as bouncers attempt to defuse the scene. *The Decline of Western Civilization* is a raw, unpolished look at a global cultural movement in its Southern California heyday, setting a new standard for music documentaries to come.

THE DECLINE OF WESTERN CIVILIZATION PART II: THE METAL YEARS

USA, 1988 • COLOR, 93 MINUTES

DIRECTOR: Penelope Spheeris

STARRING: Ozzy Osbourne, Alice Cooper, Steven Tyler, Joe Perry, Gene Simmons, Paul Stanley

The second film in Spheeris's legendary documentary trilogy *The Decline of Western Civilization I, II*, and *III* also focuses on a Los Angeles–based music scene, but instead of punk, it investigates the "glam metal" period of hard rock and heavy metal in the late 1980s. Unlike the grittiness of punk rock, glam metal celebrated excess and ostentatiousness—less anger and disillusionment, more fantasy, sex, and big hair. The documentary homes in on a handful of L.A. bands in various stages of success. Interviews with members of Poison and Faster Pussycat, bands new to national fame and commercial airplay, are intercut with stories from globally famous old-guard musicians such as Ozzy Osbourne, Alice Cooper, Steven Tyler and Joe Perry from Aerosmith, Gene Simmons and Paul Stanley from KISS, and Lemmy from Motorhead. Into this mix, Spheeris adds interviews with local bands who are striving to make it, from their nights handing out flyers for their small local club shows to their tales of having to beg women to buy them groceries.

As she did in the first *Decline* film, Spheeris talks to a wild assortment of fans, club owners, and concert promoters involved in this scene.

The tone shift between *Decline I* and *Decline II* is either welcome or horrifying, depending on how you look at it. The punks from the first documentary certainly matched the energy and bravado (and the alcohol and substance abuse) of the subjects in *Decline II*. But a visible difference between punk and glam metal is obvious from the first frames of the film. There is pageantry in glam metal: costuming, preening. Nobody is bleeding from a mosh pit injury. The women who appear alongside the band members are scantily clad, more groupies than active participants. Even the women Spheeris interviews who are musicians (a member of the all-female metal band Vixen appears in the documentary) seem to be eclipsed by the sheer machismo and hyper-masculine rock star antics that dominate the rest of the film (look no further than Paul Stanley from KISS being interviewed in

FROM TOP: Mother and son headbangers • Lemmy from Motorhead drinks a Pepsi in front of the L.A. skyline

bed with multiple women, in lingerie, staring at him lovingly). Again, Spheeris attempts to puncture some of these moments with pointed questions, a recurring one being, "but what if you don't make it?" This isn't the only time Spheeris voices a thought we're all thinking. Another infamous scene takes place during her interview with Chris Holmes from W.A.S.P. who's drunk and floating in his pool as his nonchalant mother watches from a deck chair. At one point, Spheeris, off-camera, is heard begging him to stop chugging an entire bottle of vodka in one sip. Overall, *Decline II* seems even more jaw-dropping than the first, leading us to question the longevity of both the musicians and the music they've devoted their lives to. As another unique snapshot of a craze that is long gone from mainstream culture, it's a fascinating time capsule.

Cult Connections

Just a few years after *The Decline of Western Civilization Part II: The Metal Years* was released, director Penelope Spheeris made perhaps one of the most famous Hollywood comedies about heavy metal and hard rock fans, *Wayne's World* (1992). Originating as a recurring skit on *Saturday Night Live* starring comedians Mike Myers and Dana Carvey, the film is centered around two long-haired teens, Wayne and Garth, as they produce a cable access show in their basement. Alice Cooper, who had appeared in the *Decline II* documentary, plays himself in the film.

THE DECLINE OF WESTERN CIVILIZATION
PART IIII

USA, 1998 • COLOR, 86 MINUTES

DIRECTOR: Penelope Spheeris

STARRING: Myke Chambers, Stephen Chambers, Flea, Gary Fredo, William A. Kirkley, Ron Martinez, Keith Morris, Michael Orr, Angela Torrez Parker, Rick Wilder

The world had changed drastically by the time Penelope Spheeris sought to document the next phase of the punk scene. Ten years after her 1988 second entry in *The Decline of Western Civilization* trilogy, the United States had been involved in three global conflicts, endured its deadliest act of domestic terrorism with the Oklahoma City bombing, and Princess Diana of Wales died following a motor accident. On top of that, a scandal was about to rock the nation as the forty-second president of the United States would endure an impeachment trial for sexual misconduct with an intern. The world seemed chaotic, and its dog-eat-dog attitude is reflected in Spheeris's bookend to her trilogy.

While the first film reflected a punk scene born out of general apathy and boredom, *Part II* rooted itself in the capitalism of the punk scene. Glam and heavy metal came with the long-sought lifestyle of sex, drugs, and rock and roll, and the MTV generation ate it up. But time quickly passed. As many of the kids who are featured in the opening moments of *Part III* note, they were all babies or not even conceived when the first film came out. "I was an unpaid abortion" one of the kids jokes, a line that is emblematic of the entire theme for *Part III*.

Spheeris captures a world of teenagers who fell into the gutter punk scene—where youths often chose a life of homelessness and panhandling—because they didn't see better options for themselves. They're children of abuse, neglect, and undiagnosed mental illnesses; they're ignored by politicians and social programs, harassed by cops, and many

are homeless. The only ways they know to cope are to stay buzzed, party hard, and mosh out their rage at punk shows. Despite the lack of supervision and guidance, they have a community in one another, and Spheeris captures the heart of this through her interviews with the teenagers.

Spheeris is more present and engaged in this segment of the trilogy. Her style is reminiscent of *Part I*, as opposed to the glamorous, at times laughably theatrical interviews of *Part II*. Here she uses film to capture the iconic lightbulb interviews in which her subjects sit to the right of a single hanging lightbulb as she asks questions, the camera tightly zooming in and out on the faces of the interviewees. She uses a video camera for the first time in the series in the homes and places of commune for the teens, presenting their closeness and camaraderie with natural grace, allowing us to connect deeper with the featured interviewees.

Spheeris has noted that her time working on the third film had a profound effect on her. She met the love of her life while filming and became a foster parent. The respect and empathy she felt for the subjects of this entry positively seeps through the screen, making for a thoughtful and touching watch. It would be fascinating to see another installment of this series as the times continue to change, but where it stands now as a trilogy, *The Decline of Western Civilization* is an unparalleled feat of filmmaking, reflecting a very sad reality of American society.

WILD SEED

USA, 1965 • B&W, 99 MINUTES

Michael Parks as Fargo

DIRECTOR: Brian G. Hutton **SCREENPLAY:** Lester Pine, Ike Jones (story)
STARRING: Michael Parks (Fargo), Celia Milius (Daffy Collinge), Ross
Elliott (James Collinge), Woodrow Chambliss (Mr. Simms),
Eva Novak (Mrs. Simms)

The late cult actor Michael Parks began his career in television in the early 1960s before making his way to film with *Wild Seed*, a surprisingly endearing but often overlooked drama-romance centered around the world of freight hopping, or train hopping. Parks seemed primed for the matinee idol route, as he was effortlessly handsome but also soulful; needless to say, he garnered many comparisons to James Dean. In the late 1960s he starred in the short-lived television series *Then Came Bronson*, which told the story of a man who quit his job after the death of a friend to ride his motorcycle across the country. During the era of *Easy Rider*, the show made Parks a star and counterculture hero (he also sang the theme song to the show).

Interestingly, there are some similarities between *Then Came Bronson* and *Wild Seed*, also about a man who eschews the rat race for a life on the road. In *Wild Seed* Parks plays Bill "Fargo" Warren, an orphaned, disaffected young man who spends his days traveling from town to town as a migrant worker but is effectively unhoused. Like Dean, Brando, and other young male actors of this generation, Parks played the misunderstood type well (oddly enough, Brando turned down the role of Fargo because he felt he was too old; the film was produced by Brando's own production company, by his father, Marlon Brando Sr.). But unlike the explosive Jim Stark in *Rebel Without a Cause*, Fargo was ultimately a much shadier character, at times, even dangerous. This, alongside the gorgeous black-and-white photography of the film and jazz score by Richard Markowitz, ultimately makes *Wild Seed* feel less like a Hollywood production and more in line

with the independent films of John Cassavetes, or even the French New Wave, as it slowly and contemplatively unfolds.

The story of *Wild Seed* was written by Ike Jones, the first Black graduate of UCLA's film school and one of the first Black producers in Hollywood, and TV writer Lester Pine. It was also the debut film of director Brian G. Hutton, a former actor who had made appearances in television series such as *Gunsmoke* and *Perry Mason* and in films such as *Gunfight*

THE WILD SEED OF LIFE GREW WITHIN THEM... Until something was bound to explode!

MICHAEL PARKS
CELIA KAYE

WILD SEED

screenplay by LES PINE
directed by BRIAN G. HUTTON
produced by ALBERT S. RUDDY
a Pennebaker Production / a Universal Release

at the O.K. Corral. The film's cinematography came courtesy of the great Conrad Hall, who made *Wild Seed* early in his career but would go on to make some of the best-looking films of the next few decades, including *In Cold Blood*, *Butch Cassidy and the Sundance Kid*, and *Fat City*. For the role of Fargo's opposite, Daphne, the young Celia Milius was hired. She, too, was relatively new to acting, having appeared in a handful of TV and film roles in the few years before *Wild Seed*. Daphne (also called Daffy at some points in the film; in fact, an early working title of the movie was *Daffy*) is impossibly innocent, with a sweet face and big, dark eyes that could easily draw comparisons to Natalie Wood in *Rebel Without a Cause*. Despite the fact that Milius was only two years younger than Parks (both were in their early twenties when making the film), she's almost childlike at times in *Wild Seed*, which makes the drama she experiences on the road even more harrowing.

Daphne (Milius) and Fargo (Parks) form a bond in *Wild Seed*.

The film begins with seventeen-year-old Daphne Collinge running away from home. At first, she hitchhikes and is eventually picked up by a much older man who sexually assaults her, then speeds away after she fights him off. She ends up walking to a gas station where a young man named Fargo lingers outside and begs her for money. After giving him a few bucks, he begins to ask her if she's hitchhiking, suddenly running down the entire list of potential dangers for a girl like her. He quickly offers his protection, but Daphne excuses herself to the gas station bathroom to get away. For an early scene, it's frightening, and she's right to be wary of him as he lies about seeing police officers pulling up to the gas station in order to gain her trust. Eventually when she does come out, he coaxes her to the diner next door for a meal.

While they sip coffee, Fargo tells her he's a migrant farm worker, jumping trains from place to place, with no family. She asks if he can help her try to get to Los Angeles and he agrees. The next morning Fargo launches into his first lesson in train jumping, and they successfully catch their first train out West. But Daphne proves she has a lot to learn about this life, and Fargo is never sure he wants to teach her. Even after she reveals she is going to L.A. to look for her real father, Fargo's hurt from his own orphaned past makes him unable to truly commit to tenderness toward her. As they try to push each other away, they keep realizing they need each other, especially as Daphne develops romantic feelings for Fargo. As many more dramatic events happen for them on the road, they find connection and loyalty in each other time and time again. The last few scenes in the film are surprisingly very emotional, the one where Fargo confronts Daphne's real father (played by character actor Ross Elliott) in his office in particular.

Wild Seed is a sensitive, thoughtful film, big on mood and atmosphere and with tons of talent behind it, making it a mystery as to why it's been underappreciated throughout the years. Daphne's foray into the train-jumping life feels like a glimpse into a secret society, and the dilemmas she and Fargo experience on the road seem much closer to real-life danger than most of the "teens in peril" films

of this era. The character of Fargo has way more in common with a Beat Generation bohemian than the classic Hollywood bad boys we'd seen in years past. Before airing on TCM Underground, it had only randomly played on television throughout the years and was notoriously hard to find on home video. Even after Parks was effectively rediscovered by a whole new generation after directors such as David Lynch, Quentin Tarantino, and Kevin Smith began casting him in their projects, the movie remained an oddity that was hard to find. A film ripe for rediscovery, Wild Seed is a must-see for Michael Parks fans and for anyone seeking out forgotten gems of 1960s cinema.

A Spotlight on . . . Michael Parks

Marketed as a heartthrob early in his career, actor Michael Parks (1940–2017) appeared in several films in the 1960s before making a comeback in his later years in genre pictures directed by Quentin Tarantino and Kevin Smith. Parks also worked frequently in television, both in his early years and in the 1980s and 1990s, when he had recurring roles in both *The Colbys* and the original *Twin Peaks* series. For more Michael Parks on film, check out:

Bus Riley's Back in Town (1965)

The Bible: In the Beginning (1966)

The Idol (1966)

The Happening (1967)

The Last Hard Men (1976)

The Private Files of J. Edgar Hoover (1977)

From Dusk till Dawn (1996)

Kill Bill: Volume 1 (2003)

Kill Bill: Volume 2 (2004)

Grindhouse (2007)

Red State (2011)

Django Unchained (2012)

Tusk (2014)

VISUAL DELIGHTS AND OTHER STRANGE MIND MELTERS

A mind is a terrible thing to waste. Good thing we've filled ours with images from these enigmatic, offbeat movies throughout the years. We like to think we're smarter for it. This chapter is devoted to spotlighting some of the wildest, weirdest, and downright most uncomfortable movies we've shown on TCM Underground. Some of these films are legends. Some haven't been seen by enough people, which is truly a shame. Others are what some would call "so bad they're good," but we don't believe in that language here. All these movies are simply iconic for their bold and daring visions or their psychedelic influences. Some are just so bizarre that they've stuck with us for decades, proving they've melted themselves onto our psyches where they will snugly stay forever. In a post–turn on, tune in, and drop out world, these films are the perfect late-night journey down a rabbit hole. Just be sure to remember which way is up.

BELLADONNA OF SADNESS

JAPAN, 1973 • COLOR, 86 MINUTES

Jeanne (Aiko Nagayama) gets in touch with her dark side.

DIRECTOR: Eiichi Yamamoto **SCREENPLAY:** Yoshiyuki Fukuda, Eiichi Yamamoto

STARRING: Tatsuya Nakadai (Devil), Katsuyuki Itō (Jean),

Aiko Nagayama (Jeanne / Belladonna), Shigako Shimegi (The Lord's Mistress),

Masaya Takahashi (The Lord), Natsuka Yashiro (The Witch),

Masakane Yonekura (The Priest)

Despite the popularity of Pixar films, the works of Hayao Miyazaki, and television shows like *Adventure Time* and *Rick & Morty*, there's still a bias surrounding animation and adult audiences. Often the general movie-going population thinks of animated films as cartoons that lack sophistication and depth, and it's no wonder when movie studios primarily choose to promote animated films that can be seen in theaters by families. Because of this misconception, a number of fantastic, cutting-edge animated films are overlooked by the general population, leaving these gems in the waiting, loving arms of cult movie fans.

Belladonna of Sadness is one of those movies. But don't let the animation fool you, this isn't what you'd call a typical feel-good cartoon. Tackling heavy themes of rape, mob mentality, and social damnation, *Belladonna* is a rare film that focuses on the violation of a woman and her subsequent perseverance through it in an empowering way. This stunning example of psychedelic animation is ripe for rediscovery—especially now in our post-#MeToo world—managing to ring loud and clear for a reclamation of body and soul. Even with the solemn subject matter at hand, *Belladonna* tells an emotionally charged story that's uplifting and visually intoxicating, making it one of the more hypnotic animated films of all time.

Jeanne, the heroine of *Belladonna of Sadness*, is a gorgeous woman drawn expertly by animators Hayao Nobe and Gisaburō Sugii to exaggerate her looks. Their use of precise lines, soft graphite, and gradient watercolors accentuate Jeanne's doe-like eyes, her flowing tumble of hair, and elegantly full lips. Jeanne is young and set to marry her fiancé, Jean. However, on her wedding day Jeanne is raped by the baron of her village. The malicious act by the baron forever changes Jean and Jeanne. Jean still loves his new bride, but he can't manage his own personal feelings about her attack, resulting in the breakdown of their marriage and eventually their humanity.

Alone and rejected by her husband and peers, Jeanne endures her trauma alone until a tiny figure appears in her bed one night. The small anthropomorphic being explains that he is Jeanne, having manifested into reality through her desperate cries and pleas for help. The figure bargains with Jeanne. He'll help her gain new power and strength if she

The villains have many faces.

allows it to feed on her hate and rage for its own growth. Assuming this figure is the Devil incarnate, Jeanne is conflicted between giving into her fury and suffering in silence as the status quo demands. Throughout this ordeal, Jeanne undergoes an existential metamorphosis, finding empowerment and healing within through the reawakening of her sexual pleasure, but the town isn't apt to make such a transformation easy for her.

Belladonna of Sadness was primed for success, as it was the third film in the "Animerama" trilogy, a group of animated films with mature and erotic themes made at Mushi Production studios and helmed by Japanese animator and manga artist Osamu Tezuka. A pioneering artist in Japan, Tezuka is considered the "Father of Manga" for cocreating early hand-drawn

graphic novels, including *Astro Boy*, a comic series that became Japan's first popular animated series and a precursor to anime. Tezuka's first two entries in the trilogy, *A Thousand and One Nights* and *Cleopatra*, were rated X in global markets for their strong sexual themes. The former was met with praise and financial success in the Japanese market, while the latter received a lukewarm response. Tezuka left production early on for *Belladonna of Sadness*, leaving his trilogy collaborator, director Eiichi Yamamoto, to work on the project with writer Yoshiyuki Fukuda. Fukuda based the story on *La Sorcière*, an 1862 book on witchcraft by Jules Michelet.

Despite the film's promising marketable elements in the 1970s—the rising interest in witchcraft, the burgeoning second wave of feminism, and a global storytelling

Tortured and abused, Jeanne is down but not out.

~~focus~~ *Belladonna of Sadness* did not find its audience. It was entered into the Berlin International Film Festival but resulted in patrons leaving the screening in droves after bringing their children to what they expected was a family film. *Belladonna of Sadness* fell into obscurity for decades, until about thirty years after its release, when it was screened at various theaters in the United States, Europe, and Japan. By the late 2010s, the initial spark of interest in *Belladonna of Sadness* swelled into a roaring flame as cult movie lovers and animation enthusiasts openly embraced it. It screened at various festivals and in 2016 received a 4k digital restoration, making it a word-of-mouth sensation. Today, *Belladonna of Sadness* feels fresh and arguably more relevant in the 2020s. Women's rights, paganistic themes, a focus on healing from trauma, and a generational appreciation for anime makes *Belladonna of Sadness* a must-see.

Genre-ly Speaking

Featuring a wide range of topics, themes, and styles, these are a collection of candy-colored animation with a dark, twisted, and/or psychedelic angle made with adults in mind: Isao Takahata's *Grave of the Fireflies* (1988), Sastoshi Kon's *Perfect Blue* (1997), Katsuhiro Ōtomo's *Akira* (1988), *Fantastic Planet* (1973), *Coonskin* (1975), *Bebe's Kids* (1992), *The Point* (1972).

HOUSE
(A.K.A. HAUSU)

JAPAN, 1977 • COLOR, 96 MINUTES

Gorgeous's aunt (Yōko Minamida) is ready for a showdown.

DIRECTOR: Nobuhiko Ōbayashi **SCREENPLAY:** Chiho Katsura, Chigumi Ōbayashi

STARRING: Kimiko Ikegami (Gorgeous), Miki Jinbo (Kung Fu), Kumiko Ohba (Fantasy), Ai Matsubara (Gari / Prof), Mieko Satō (Mac), Eriko Tanaka (Melody), Masayo Miyako (Sweet), Yōko Minamida (Auntie)

*H*ouse is a cinematic experience like no other. Director Nobuhiko Ōbayashi created a film so bizarre and surreal that it feels like a fever dream, mostly because it's a patchwork of influences from the experimental, underground film scene to Ōbayashi's young daughter's own imagination. *House* at times feels like a psychological personality test that should be studied on a PhD level—or at least shown at more midnight screenings so new audiences can howl in laughter with it

As far as plot goes, the loose story follows a group of schoolgirls whose summer plans are put through the ringer when Gorgeous, frustrated that her widowed father is marrying a new woman, invites her friends to her late mother's childhood home in the countryside. The home is now occupied by her estranged aunt, who happily accepts the visitors.

Embarking on their journey with innocent giggles, cotton-candied sweetness, and sunny ideas of playing hide-and-seek in mind, they soon discover there is something amiss with the old house and Gorgeous's aunt, and one by one the demonic house begins picking off its victims. The story stays relatively simple even when the motives and actions are beyond complex. Gorgeous, Fantasy, Mac (short for Stomach), Melody, Prof (short for Professor), Kung Fu, and Sweet are characters that embody the names given to them. We don't need nuances in this story, just archetypes to play with, which makes the overall humor of the film that much more on-the-nose and bonkers.

Billed as a horror comedy, *House* is a genre mash-up that defies every rule you thought existed for cinema and narrative structure.

To call it a horror film is way too limiting. It's an experimental film first, a comedy second. It's also fantasy, melodrama, parody, partially a musical, and at times it feels like a collage of commercials, too. This is all thanks to the creative freedom granted to Ōbayashi for his feature-length debut. Possessing a childhood fondness for art, he began making films at an early age before developing into an experimental filmmaker working primarily with 8mm and 16mm. While developing his craft, he worked in a collective with several pioneering counterculture directors through the 1960s and soon after started working in

Gorgeous's aunt has a bit of an issue.

FROM LEFT: The House takes another victim. • Fantasy (Kumiko Ohba) finds a surprise in the well.

television, eventually making a staggering three thousand commercials in his career.

It took famed Japanese production company Toho Studios to come calling for the director to finally make a feature. Known for their success with *kaiju* movies, more specifically the *Godzilla* franchise, as well as films directed by the legendary Akira Kurosawa, Toho was in a precarious situation during the late 1970s. The studio had witnessed the success of Steven Spielberg's *Jaws* (1975) and approached Ōbayashi to write a script for a film that could

be the studio's *Jaws*. Ōbayashi went to his adolescent daughter, Chigumi Ōbayashi, for ideas and turned her horror fantasy scenarios over to screenplay writer Chiho Katsura. The finished script sat untouched for two years, as no director at Toho wanted their names attached to the eccentric project. Ōbayashi instead took the idea and made a manga and a successful radio drama out of it before Toho gave him the green light to direct it.

Employing a host of mostly untrained models as his stars, Ōbayashi also used family members and friends throughout the production, including Chigumi as the on-set scenarist. The creative freedom and ragtag production style are palpable through the screen. *House* is an assault on the senses that manages to go overboard while not being overbearing. It's filled with silly sight gags and goofball jokes that are just cheesy enough to make you laugh—and occasionally even spit take. Sometimes, it's obviously intentional, like when a haunted skeleton dances in the background of a few scenes or a character eats a watermelon and reveals to Fantasy that it's really an eyeball (the poor girl will need a psychiatrist after the trauma she is put through here). Other times, we're not so sure the humor is intentional, such as when there are repetitive seagull calls during a dramatic scene or the strange, off-kilter music cues that sound like the skeleton may be playing piano even before we meet him.

There's an abandonment of form and logic in *House* that helps it stand out as a cult classic and is the reason it's become so beloved among underground movie fans. It's self-aware but also genuinely attempts to be unique in its artistry. There are shots that are beautifully framed with perfect composition, reminding viewers that there is a skilled artist behind the camera. Ōbayashi uses every trick in the editing handbook to dizzying effect, like when characters dissolve into others or pinholes point out important moments that he wants to make sure aren't overlooked by viewers. These embellishments are hysterical when they happen, which is part of the film's charm.

Surprisingly for everyone involved, the film was a box-office success in Japan, though critics panned it. It gained a following in Japan through young audience members, but it would take more than thirty years before *House* premiered in theaters across America. In true underground fashion, these limited screenings and word of mouth helped the film gain its prized status as a treasured cult classic across the globe.

WTF Moment

If feels almost like cheating to grant this film a WTF Moment, considering the entire runtime of *House* is devoted to being outlandish. However, we'd be remiss if we didn't mention a truly outstanding moment: the reveal of a possessed Gorgeous while Melody plays a possessed piano. The scene rapidly shifts from its mystery of finding Gorgeous, to scary and hilarious wonder all at once when the house takes over and Melody can no longer control her playing. The piano eats her fingers, then her hands, then ultimately her entire body. Limbs are tossed and distorted as the music now plays rapidly off-key. Melody teeters back and forth between frenzied laughter and fear as she looks at her dismembered body. Poor Fantasy witnesses the carnage happening before her eyes while the house skeleton dances in excitement in the background. It's a sensational moment in cinematic history.

MAC AND ME

USA, 1988 • COLOR, 99 MINUTES

Actors Jade Calegory and Lauren Stanley with their otherworldly costar

DIRECTOR: Stewart Raffill   **SCREENPLAY:** Stewart Raffill, Steve Feke

STARRING: Christine Ebersole (Janet Cruise), Jonathan Ward (Michael Cruise), Tina Caspary (Courtney), Lauren Stanley (Debbie), Jade Calegory (Eric Cruise), Vinnie Torrente (Mitford), Martin West (Wickett), Ivan J. Rado (Zimmerman), Danny Cooksey (Jack Jr.)

For a certain group of Millennial and Gen-X kids, *Mac and Me* is legendary. Whether you think it's a train wreck or misunderstood gold (no one thinks that, mind you), it's likely that you've seen this movie on either cable television or on VHS at a sleepover. Since then, *Mac and Me*'s notoriety has only grown. Even if you've never seen the film before, it's likely you've seen the iconic clip from *Mac and Me* involving a young boy in a wheelchair rolling frantically down a hill, over a waterfall, and into a body of water while a poorly designed alien looks at the rear-projection action that just took place. That scene became a popular meme and a hilarious recurring prank on Conan O'Brien's former *Late Night* talk show by actor Paul Rudd. The film itself—aired on TCM Underground and appearing on *Mystery Science Theater 3000*—has become celebrated with screenings and cosplay and is frequently considered one of the worst films ever made. No wonder it's become a cult classic.

Mac and Me could have been a heartfelt, progressive sci-fi film, but instead of being an homage to Steven Spielberg's blockbuster *E.T. the Extra-Terrestrial* (1982), it instead became a hollow gimmick intended to exploit its young audience by substituting overt product placement for a meaningful plot. Having previously worked in advertising for McDonald's, the film's producer, R. J. Louis, who had just scored back-to-back hits as executive producer on *The Karate Kid* (1984) and *The Next Karate Kid* (1986), came up with the concept for *Mac and Me* after determining that the two most popular icons for children at the time were Ronald McDonald and E.T. With this logic in mind, it

only made sense to throw money at creating a feature film that showcased both.

In an attempt to avoid making the alien, Mac (whose name is an acronym for Mysterious Alien Creature, but more importantly, short for Big Mac), a complete rip-off of E.T., the creators of the film decided that Mac would have a family . . . you know, because E.T. didn't. Director Stewart Raffill was brought into the production, to his surprise, after the crew had already been hired. When he asked Louis about the script, Raffill was informed that he'd have to write it quickly and on weekends in between prepping for filming. This led to a screenplay in which the emotions don't translate, mostly because the aliens don't make sense. In fact,

CLOCKWISE FROM TOP LEFT: Ronald McDonald in his first and only film appearance • The starry-eyed protagonist • Actor Jade Calegory rides down a hill in this infamous scene.

sense doesn't have much skin in the game with *Mac and Me*. The odd camera angles, the poorly directed action sequences, the even shoddier editing, the amount of product placement present in this movie—all are absolutely nonsensical. But these elements only skim the surface of what makes this a historically bad but shockingly awesome picture.

We'd argue that *Mac and Me* is in a tiny genre of its own: body horror comedy. This movie is horrific from the onset when we first meet the alien family (perhaps on the moon, although their location is never really established . . . just space). While E.T. undoubtedly freaked out some children due to its alien texture, it was a charming creature with enough human traits to elicit an empathetic emotion from even the most passive viewer. The aliens of *Mac and Me*, however, are apt to terrify nearly every audience member, as they are frankly disgusting. Fat-jowled, sickly thin, with demonic, vacant eyes and skin that's simultaneously taut, rubbery, and claylike, they have the makings of a dreadful nightmare. What's more, these creatures surprisingly become more unappealing with every new shot that reveals more of their bodies, covered in liver spots, scaly appendages, and cracked elbows.

Mac and Me is jaw-droppingly bad—a hoot to watch alone, but practically required viewing with an audience. There are many moments that are better when shared, like the fantastically puzzling grocery store shootout scene or the wild highway car-chase sequences. Somehow this movie only gets worse (or better, in a so-bad-it's-good way) as its runtime wanes, and yet it still manages to be boring and lifeless.

Did we mention the rampant product placement in this movie? Skittles, NASA, Coke, Dos Equis, Energizer, Snorks, Brawny—if it had a brand name in the 1980s, then it likely appears in this movie. It's the *Ready Player One* and *Wreck It Ralph* for consumer products. *Mac and Me*'s production sparked a bidding war of sorts with Disney, which fought for exclusive rights to partner with McDonald's. The film was meant to be a profitable agreement for Ronald McDonald House Charities, but It tanked, making only $6 million of its $13 million budget. If nothing else good came from *Mac and Me*, at least Millennials and Gen-Xers got Disney-inspired toys in their Happy Meals for nearly twenty years to come.

OMG Moment

This entire movie is an OMG moment, but nothing can prepare you for the truly bizarre McDonald's musical commercial that interrupts the film for no natural reason. Complete with every '80s stereotype (break-dancers, bad outfits, teddy bears, aerobics-style dancing, Ronald McDonald in the flesh), the sequence manages to be shocking, entertaining, unsettling, and mundane all at once. *Mac and Me* exists in a world of frightening uncanniness, but watching Mac dance in an awful teddy bear suit with those rubbery, large eyes peering at us from within is simply frightening. Nothing about this scene makes sense and it only gets worse (better) with each passing minute. Thank the movie gods for that!

SATANIS: THE DEVIL'S MASS

USA, 1970 • COLOR, 86 MINUTES

LaVey, the leader of the Church of Satan

DIRECTOR: Ray Laurent

STARRING: Anton LaVey, Diane LaVey, Karla LaVey, Isaac Bonewits

When the author/musician/occultist Anton LaVey officially began the Church of Satan in 1966, he likely found no better place in America that would possibly be receptive to his new doctrine than San Francisco. The spirit of the 1849 Gold Rush was embedded deep into the history of California, and the city had been a hotbed for countercultural ideals ever since the Beats began congregating there post–World War II. It was around that time that LaVey purchased a home in the city that would be known as the Black House for the simple fact that its outside was entirely painted black. LaVey regularly held salons there discussing a variety of occult subjects including magic, hypnosis, and witchcraft. Its participants would be dubbed the Magic Circle and were said to include people from all walks of life, even prominent members of academia and police officers. LaVey was laying the groundwork for what would become the formal tenets of the Church, which he collected and published as *The Satanic Bible* in 1969.

Roman Polanski's film *Rosemary's Baby* was a hit the year before, resulting in a sudden interest in the occult and Satanism. LaVey was rumored to have been a consultant on the movie, and he claimed to have played the beast during the famous impregnation

LaVey at home in the Black House

LaVey holds court in his famous cape.

a forbidden world for the express interest of shock and awe. The documentary is primarily footage of a black mass being held by LaVey and his congregation, but also collects interviews from several different sources including LaVey himself (his wife and daughter are also interviewed), assorted church members, and LaVey's neighbors in San Francisco who live near the infamous Black House, unaffiliated with the group. As the master of ceremonies, LaVey, in his signature look (bald with a black goatee), makes his first appearance in a black-hooded robe with tiny horns protruding from the top. An organ plays softly in the background as an assortment of ritualistic iconography pops in and out of frame including cloaks, skull and devil masks, live snakes and swords, and, of course, naked women posed at the altar. The ambient red lighting and the low Dutch angles make the scenes even more dramatic.

We later see a one-on-one interview with LaVey as he attempts to explain the tenets of Satanism, which value personal freedom and expression above all else. Other members of the church are also interviewed and seem to be varied in age (though mostly white). One of the most entertaining conversations is with a much older woman of the church, who looked like anyone's grandmother except with a giant pentacle necklace dangling from her neck. She mentions getting into Satanism via her interest in witchcraft, how she's very much into nature, laughs when she replies she decided to own dogs instead of have children, and takes long drags off her cigarette while smiling. Another middle-aged woman of the church is interviewed naked with a skull covering her vagina, talking freely about masturbation and passing

scene (though his name does not appear in the movie's credits). Hollywood soon began ringing the bell at The Black House, including visits from celebrities such as Jayne Mansfield and Sammy Davis Jr. LaVey had been officially thrust in the national spotlight a few years earlier after performing a Satanic marriage for socialite Judith Case and the journalist John Raymond and performed the first Satanic baptism on his own daughter, which caused a worldwide stir (and was recorded for an album called *The Satanic Mass*). There was much momentum, then, for a documentary about LaVey and his church, produced and directed by the editor Ray Laurent, called *Satanis: The Devil's Mass*.

From the outside, *Satanis* has all the trappings of a mondo film, promising a peek into

gas. When you consider their lifestyles would have been seen as radical in this day and age, their interview answers make these women seem almost ahead of their time. Another interesting moment of the documentary is seeing the church members sitting alongside LaVey discussing their beliefs, including their dogma on sexual freedom, homosexuality, and general sex positivity, with LaVey underscoring the acceptance of any and all sexual desires and fetishes within the church. There are others, however, who see the members as strange and slightly dangerous, and in *Satanis* they are also given the spotlight. A big topic of conversation was centered around the LaVey family owning a real lion that they named Togare and raised in the Black House. Certain members of the neighborhood, fearful of the great beast and intolerant of the animal noises coming from the house, went to the authorities. The family was eventually forced to turn the lion over to the local zoo but allegedly the family placed a curse on everyone who participated in the protest. On the other hand, some seem to be more of a mixed bag of both judgment and curiosity. LaVey's direct next-door neighbor, wearing an entirely pink outfit next to her child (also in all pink), even seems to be slightly amused by the goings-on in the Black House.

Much of the intrigue and outright entertainment of *Satanis: The Devil's Mass* comes simply from the passage of time. The black mass scenes seem slightly funny by today's standards, much like a kitschy Halloween play. LaVey himself also seems less the representation of pure evil and more an avid collector of gothic items, dark paintings, and spooky ephemera. As the leader of the

Satanic Church until his death in 1997, LaVey was steadily covered in the press, who were keen to invoke him during moments of moral crisis. Interestingly enough, clips of *Satanis* were often used during news magazine shows such as *20/20* and in special reports by talk show hosts such as Geraldo Rivera during the Satanic Panic era of the 1980s. (LaVey himself would also appear as a guest on these shows.) In the 1970s, however, the documentary was essentially pushed into obscurity after failing to get major, national distribution upon release. Conveniently, when it did manage to screen, it often shared a bill alongside Kenneth Anger's experimental short *Invocation of My Demon Brother* (1969), a film where LaVey himself played the role of "His Satanic Majesty." As a document of an outré society and a piece of San Franciscan history, *Satanis* is devilishly entertaining.

Cult Connections

The experimental director Kenneth Anger has ties to several people and films mentioned in this book, including LaVey, the occultist/artist Marjorie Cameron of *The Wormwood Star* fame, and the director Curtis Harrington. Appearing alongside LaVey in Anger's *Invocation of My Demon Brother* are Bobby Beausoleil, who would later join the Manson Family (and receive a life sentence after murdering Manson associate Gary Hinman), and Mick Jagger, lead singer of the Rolling Stones.

THE GARBAGE PAIL KIDS MOVIE

USA, 1987 • COLOR, 100 MINUTES

Captain Manzini (Anthony Newley) with the Kids

DIRECTOR: Rod Amateau   **SCREENPLAY:** Linda Palmer, Rod Amateau, John Pound

STARRING: Anthony Newley (Captain Manzini), Mackenzie Astin (Dodger),
Phil Fondacaro (Greaser Greg), Katie Barberi (Tangerine),
Debbie Lee Carrington (Valerie Vomit)

We who work on TCM Underground are generally unflappable when it comes to our consumption of oddball films, but the limits were definitely tested when we aired one of the most notorious and storied films of the 1980s, *The Garbage Pail Kids Movie*. Based on a series of popular trading cards made by the Topps Corporation, the film was one of several based on popular children's toys of the decade. The 1980s were a golden era for both toy manufacturers and the children's entertainment business, and a proliferation of motion pictures based on the story lines and mythologies of some of the highest-selling action figures and dolls appeared, including *The Care Bears Movie* (1985), *Transformers: The Movie* (1986), *My Little Pony: The Movie* (1986), and *Masters of the Universe* (1987). The Garbage Pail Kids cards were a mischievous take on the sweet and cuddly, soft-bodied Cabbage Patch Kids dolls created by Xavier Roberts, which had caused a sensation when they launched in 1982. The Garbage Pail Kids were warped versions of the original dolls, usually suffering from an unfortunate physical situation (vomiting, farting, acne) or tragedy (electrocution, a spider attack, an atomic bomb planted in the brain). They, too, would become a sensation among kids, which of course meant Hollywood came calling. The resulting movie, however, achieved none of the success that the cards had.

Director/writer Rod Amateau, who had spent decades in film and directing episodes of classic television shows like *Gilligan's Island* and *Mister Ed*, was nearing the end of his career and was looking to take on a project that would earn him enough money to retire from the business. Amateau purchased the rights to the Garbage Pail Kids to make into a TV movie, and he penned a script with co-writer Linda Palmer. Unfamiliar with the history of the cards and with little to no input from Topps, Amateau roughed out a story, scraped up a threadbare budget, and filming began. Cast as the lead character, the fourteen-year-old Dodger, was Mackenzie Astin, son of the famous Hollywood couple John Astin and Patty Duke. The role of the adult in the film, the kind and slightly wacky antique store owner Captain Manzini, went to British actor/musician Anthony Newley. Cast as the Garbage Pail Kids themselves were a series of professional little person actors who were required to wear extremely uncomfortable character suits with animatronic heads controlled by a special effects team. The doll heads were so cumbersome and fragile that they were virtually impossible to film for more than minutes at a time, and blocked out all sight and sound for the performers wearing

It came from outer space.

FROM TOP: Katie Barberi and Mackenzie Astin • Juice (Ron MacLachlan) gets squeezed by the Garbage Pail Kids.

them (actor Arturo Gil recalls knocking into set pieces and having to scream his lines any time his was worn).

The film itself treads a somewhat predictable plot that follows similar beats established by popular '80s films such as *E.T.* and *Gremlins*. The Garbage Pail Kids, hailing from outer space (no other details beyond that fact), have somehow landed their trash can on Earth inside an antique store and are one day accidentally released by Dodger. Captain Manzini quickly admonishes him for doing so, telling him they need to be hidden from the public at all costs for fear of the "normies" misunderstanding their vast differences. The kids immediately start causing trouble (each as per their unique personality), donning disguises to go out in public, behaving obnoxiously, and starting a fight in a biker bar (in an especially memorable moment, one of the bikers has his mustache blown off by a fart released by one of the kids). Eventually, they are discovered by the town bully, Juice (Ron MacLachlan), and he helps the kids get sent to a nefarious institution called the State Home for the Ugly, where they will be locked away and eventually killed for being too unattractive and gross to exist. With the help of Tangerine (Barberi), a young fashion designer that Dodger also has a crush on, the Garbage Pail Kids are ceremoniously busted out of the home to spread the message of kindness and tolerance while also continuing in their naughty ways.

Unfortunately for *The Garbage Pail Kids Movie*, kindness and tolerance were not given toward the film, which opened in very limited release in August 1987 and was panned almost instantly. In the *New York Times*, film critic Caryn James said, "*The Garbage Pail Kids Movie* is enough to make you believe in strict and faraway boarding schools." Whether it was the formulaic plot, the absurdity of the story line, the disgusting visual sight gags of the kids vomiting, farting, and snacking on severed fingers and toes, or just the plain fact that the animatronic doll faces were *incredibly creepy*, the movie ended up on several Worst Movie Lists of the year and was promptly shelved. Over the years, however, cult movie audiences have plucked the film out of obscurity and have given it a new life, to the extent that the Tornante Company (owned by ex-Disney CEO Michael Eisner) considered a reboot in 2012 (it was eventually put to rest). *The Garbage Pail Kids Movie* is a fascinating relic of an era dominated by youth consumerism and is worth viewing, whether fueled by childhood nostalgia, sheer curiosity, or pure awe that such a film exists.

OMG Moment

In a movie that trucks in the feeling of "What am I watching?!" at virtually every turn, one of the most interesting concepts the film presents is the State Home for the Ugly, designed as a place for the hideous and undesired. When the Garbage Pail Kids arrive at the home, they notice several famous faces who have already been jailed: Abraham Lincoln, who is deemed Too Skinny; Santa Claus, who is noted as Too Fat; and, extra puzzling, Mahatma Gandhi, who is Too Bald.

THE WORLD'S GREATEST SINNER

USA, 1962 • B&W, 77 MINUTES

Timothy Carey as Clarence "God" Hilliard

DIRECTOR: Timothy Carey   **SCREENPLAY:** Timothy Carey

STARRING: Timothy Carey (Clarence Hilliard), Gil Barreto (Alonzo), Betty Rowland (Edna Hilliard), James Farley (The Devil), Gail Griffin (Betty Hilliard)

Character actor Timothy Carey became a beloved and cherished figure among film fans for his ability to take a bit part in a famous movie and make a lasting impression: the sharpshooter that gunned down a racehorse in Stanley Kubrick's *The Killing*, the sobbing soldier sentenced to death in *Paths of Glory*, a beer-throwing biker in *The Wild One*. Off-screen he was larger than life, both in appearance (tall with dark hair and big, emotional eyes) and in personality, where alleged incidents with his costars have become the stuff of Hollywood legend. Kirk Douglas reportedly hated his guts. He was rumored to have been beaten up by Richard Widmark on the set of *The Last Wagon* and nearly choked by Seymour Cassel in *The Killing of a Chinese Bookie*. Another story has Carey convincing the director/actor John Cassavetes to put on a suit designed to sustain a dog attack and let three Rottweilers jump on him. A notorious prankster, he once climbed into the trunk of a car to be thrown from the Santa Monica Pier just to get attention. People would sometimes flirt with the idea of hiring him just to see what would happen, as was reportedly the case during the preproduction of *River's Edge* (he did not get the part). The actor himself claimed he was "probably fired more than any other actor in Hollywood."

Born in Brooklyn, New York, in 1929, to a close-knit Italian family, Carey used the GI Bill to attend drama school. His first movies were small roles in the noir film *Crime Wave* and in the epic *East of Eden* (where he played the small but memorable role as the bouncer in the brothel where James Dean's mother

works). However, somewhere in the mid-to-late 1950s, Carey desired to make his own picture, over which he had complete control, as a vehicle to showcase his talent. He was unafraid of doing a controversial film, one

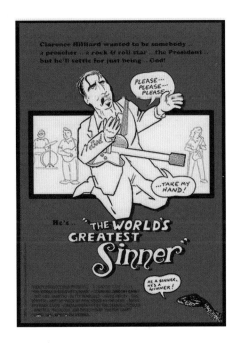

that tackled a variety of contentious topics: religion, politics, corruption, stardom, rock and roll, life, and death. It was called *The World's Greatest Sinner*, a movie both ahead of its time in subject and in production (it was written, directed, produced, and distributed by Carey himself). At its center is Clarence Hilliard (played by Carey), an insurance salesman and family man who decides one day that his job is meaningless and promptly quits. After seeing a rockabilly band perform, he decides to take up guitar with the express interest of becoming a rock star. With the help of his gardener (Gil Barreto) and under the advice of Satan (in the form of a snake), Clarence begins to hold public rallies, calling for people to join his newly formed Eternal Man Party, promising that they will become "superhuman beings" and never die. He quickly seduces an elderly woman for money (getting into a hot-and-heavy make-out session with her), applies a fake goatee to his face, and starts calling himself God.

As God, he begins to perform concerts for his newly acquired fans, wearing a gold lamé suit reminiscent of Elvis, gyrating and thrashing, and pleading to the crowd, "Please! Please! Please! Take . . . my . . . hand!" The audience goes absolutely bonkers, throwing themselves at him in hysterical glee, and soon they begin wearing armbands with the letter F written on them (for "follower"). His power and influence grow, eventually to the point where his disciples have even begun killing themselves in his name. God begins to make huge headlines across the country, deciding eventually to run for public office, but he has already become so popular with the country that he's essentially a dictator, having dalliances with young women and spreading chaos across the land. By the film's end, God has an epic showdown with the *actual* God to decide the fate of the world.

Needless to say, *The World's Greatest Sinner* is a strange and awesome piece of outsider art. From the handcrafted shots to the epic performance of Clarence "God" Hilliard, the movie is a true passion project: one man's singular vision to the very end. The musical scenes are especially fun, with Carey shaking like a possessed madman, never concerned with anything but committing to the

performance. Minute by minute, the film gets weirder and weirder, especially as Carey dons the fake facial hair and communicates with Satan-as-snake. Magnificently, it somehow stays semi-coherent even as it wanders off the edge.

Carey was incredibly proud of the film, but it never secured wide theatrical distribution after its limited release in 1962. As it was never officially released on home video and theatrical screenings were few and far between, the film has become a true underground classic over the years. Carey would periodically return to the film, using money earned from his acting work as well as his frequent guest appearances on television to fund re-edits and the shooting of new scenes (he managed to get a sponsorship of $25,000 from M. A. Ripps, the producer of another Carey film, *Bayou*, a.k.a. *Poor White Trash*). What little outside help he did have for *The World's Greatest Sinner* came from two notable cult icons: a young Frank Zappa, whom Carey hired to write the theme song, and Ray Dennis Steckler, who would go on to become a legendary B-moviemaker in his own right, serving as cinematographer. In his later years, Carey *still* handled all distribution of the film, personally bringing prints to theaters that would screen it (his son Romeo carries on the tradition). Carey passed away in 1994 from a stroke, but his legacy as one of cinema's most notorious wild men continues to this day.

OPPOSITE: The great character actor Timothy Carey

A Spotlight on . . . Timothy Carey

There's no doubt even the most casual movie fan has seen Timothy Carey (1929–1994) in a movie and not even realized it (though we find that impossible). He appeared in almost one hundred films and television shows throughout his entire career, often times uncredited but still managing to make a scene. Check out this list of some of his most memorable appearances and see if you can spot him:

Ace in the Hole (1951)	*Paths of Glory* (1957)
Crime Wave (1953)	*One-Eyed Jacks* (1961)
The Wild One (1953)	*Beach Blanket Bingo* (1965)
East of Eden (1955)	*Head* (1968)
The Killing (1956)	*What's the Matter with Helen?* (1971)
Bayou (1957)	*Minnie and Moskowitz* (1971)

THE WORMWOOD STAR

USA, 1956 • COLOR, 10 MINUTES

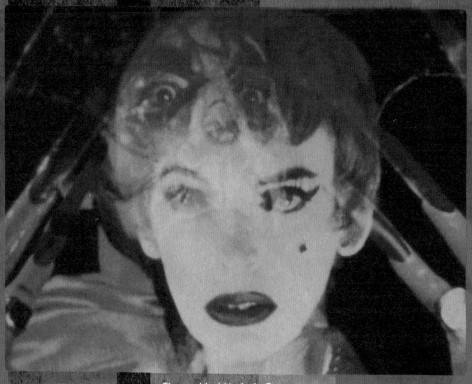

The mythical Marjorie Cameron

DIRECTOR: Curtis Harrington   **SCREENPLAY:** Curtis Harrington

STARRING: Marjorie Cameron (The Woman)

The visual artist/poet/actress Marjorie Cameron became a countercultural icon starting in the 1950s for her affiliation with the rocket scientist and Jet Propulsion Laboratories cofounder, Jack Parsons. Parsons was a member of a new religious movement called Thelema, originated by the writer/occultist Aleister Crowley in 1904. Dedicated to a strict belief in individualism, following one's "true life path," and using sexual intercourse for magical purposes, Parsons had gathered followers of Thelema in his Pasadena mansion, which became a bohemian commune of artists, free-thinkers, and free-lovers. Cameron had moved to California after a stint in the US Navy, following family

members who took jobs at JPL. When Parsons met Cameron, he was convinced she was the "elemental woman" he had summoned to the house during an invoking ritual called "The Babalon Working" (famously, Parsons had completed this ritual alongside the author and Scientology founder L. Ron Hubbard). Cameron and Parsons were soon married and lived together until his accidental death by lab explosion in 1952. After her husband's passing, Cameron continued her interest in esoteric ideas and higher spiritual consciousness. She moved in circles with members of the Beat Generation, spent many years in the Californian desert concentrating on her art, took psychedelic drugs, and befriended several

A surreal image from the film

Cameron up close

like-minded artists in Los Angeles, including experimental filmmaker and author Kenneth Anger, actors Dean Stockwell and Dennis Hopper, collage artist Wallace Berman, and director Curtis Harrington. Cameron would thus become a muse and mentor to many in the L.A. art scene, and it wasn't long before Harrington wanted to work with her on a film.

Born and raised in Los Angeles, Harrington attended USC and immediately began making his first films in the early 1940s. After penning an index about his hero, the Austrian American director Josef von Sternberg, Harrington made several experimental shorts including the fourteen-minute, black-and-white *Fragment of Seeking* (1946), in which the director himself plays a young man on a contemplative search for romance, and the beachy, windswept *Picnic* (1949), featuring Harrington's real mother

and father in lead roles. Harrington would also serve as cinematographer on fellow filmmaker Anger's film *Puce Moment* (1949) and also act alongside Cameron in one of Anger's seminal works, *Inauguration of the Pleasure Dome* (1954). Harrington was a fan of Marjorie Cameron's evocative, surrealist paintings, and his short film *The Wormwood Star* is both a showcase for her pieces and a tribute to the enigmatic woman.

Clocking in at roughly ten minutes, the film begins with hand-drawn title cards before dissolving into a dreamlike assemblage of images: Cameron draped in red and purple cloths, tight close-up shots of her face, roses, and ritualistic iconography. The camera captures her short, cropped haircut and intense stare before moving toward the bottom portion of her face, where she is resplendent in bright orange-red lipstick. Cameron begins to recite a poem as pictures of her drawings are flashed on-screen, each with a haunted, slightly spooky vibe. The drawings are intricate, mostly of bodies and faces: a womb, a younger person (perhaps a child), a man without eyes. The images suddenly shift from black-and-white to color, now with deep reds and blues, and figures of birds and other winged creatures. Suddenly, Cameron returns, wrapped in gold and crowned in a circle of gold leaves, as she stares into the camera to close out the film.

Haunting and poetic, *The Wormwood Star* seems more in line with the psychedelic films of the 1960s than something that was made in the previous decade. Cameron's lack of facial expressions during the close-up shots is intense and slightly spooky and makes the entire film feel as if you're slowly falling under her spell. Harrington would work with Cameron again a few years later on his very first feature-length film, *Night Tide* (1961). A fantasy-romance-mystery set in Santa Monica, California, and starring Dennis Hopper (in his first starring role) as a sailor who finds himself in love with a sideshow mermaid, Cameron plays a mythical being known as the Sea Witch, who appears to Hopper's character intermittently (she has zero lines of dialogue in the film). Harrington would go on to a prolific career in television and make several Hollywood films including *Games* featuring Simone Signoret and James Caan, and two starring the classic actress Shelley Winters: *What's the Matter with Helen?* and *Whoever Slew Auntie Roo?* However, Harrington's early work has only recently been made available. *The Wormwood Star* was almost completely unavailable for many years after its release, and most of Cameron's works featured in the film were destroyed by the artist herself, making Cameron a bit of an underground legend by the time of her death in 1995. Her popularity has certainly grown since the advent of the internet, however, with access to her films and surviving paintings growing steadily. Additionally, recent interest in the life of Jack Parsons via biographical television shows and musicals has also made Cameron's name more famous, introducing her legacy to a whole new generation.

A Spotlight on . . . Curtis Harrington

Curtis Harrington had an incredible career that spanned decades, yielding some of the most interesting films of the last half of the twentieth century. As a queer filmmaker who began in the Los Angeles avant-garde scene but made a big leap to Hollywood, Harrington imbued even his bigger budget projects with quirky and slightly subversive tones. For more, check out the following:

Night Tide (1961)

Queen of Blood (1966)

What's the Matter with Helen? (1971)

Whoever Slew Auntie Roo? (1971)

Devil Dog: The Hound of Hell (TV movie, 1978)

XANADU

USA, 1980 • COLOR, 96 MINUTES

A muse and her artist on roller skates

DIRECTOR: Robert Greenwald
SCREENPLAY: Richard Christian Danus, Marc Reid Rubel
STARRING: Olivia Newton-John (Kira), Gene Kelly (Danny McGuire),
Michael Beck (Sonny Malone), James Sloyan (Simpson), Dimitra Arliss
(Helen), Katie Hanley (Sandra), Fred McCarren (Richie), Renn Woods (Jo)

It's hard for us to write about this movie and not scream its praises to the heavens, or to remain objective about its brilliance. Although commonly considered a bomb, *Xanadu* is one of our favorite late-night watches. Sure, it's a *mess*, if you're judging it from a perspective of standard Hollywood fare. The story makes little to no sense. The performances leave much to be desired. Gene Kelly is obviously in a completely different film from everyone else. And yes, it all feels like a disjointed, cocaine-fueled splatter of spaghetti thrown against the wall. Instead of picking one thing or the other, the makers of this film took everything that stuck, and it seems there's nothing from any draft of the script that didn't stick. They then mixed it into a pot, adding too many contrasting spices (is that creamy grapefruit I taste?), but the resulting concoction is a delicacy of rare proportions. There's fire and ice, salty and sweet, tangy and bitter, there's a loose peppercorn floating around, and it's absolutely delightful!

Let us paint you a picture of this film's brilliance: there's roller-skating Olivia Newton-John, a Day-Glo color scheme, Electric Light Orchestra's Jeff Lynne pouring melodic sunshine into every song, a rock-versus-swing battle between the 1940s and the '80s, plus cowboys, punks, candy stripers . . . you name it, this movie has it all! It's easy to roll your eyes at this hodgepodge of elements, assuming *Xanadu* is one of those films that can be written off because it's subjectively considered so bad it's good. We are here to tell you this film really isn't bad. It's a misunderstood carnival ride, and once you watch it through its cotton candy daze, you'll feel every bit of

Kira (Olivia Newton John) and Sonny Malone (Michael Beck) share a down-home moment.

Michael Beck and Olivia Newton-John look at the film's true star.

the high with only a slightly sugary sickness afterward. If you feel that after watching it, just relisten to the soundtrack, an undeniably fabulous power-pop masterpiece.

Xanadu wasn't meant to be the big-budget picture it became. It began as a low-budget roller disco flick meant to capitalize on the late-'70s fad. However, when Olivia Newton-John signed as the lead, the budget shot up due to her soaring popularity after the success of *Grease* (1978). Soon after, Gene Kelly was added to the roster in what would be his final dramatic role, and Michael Beck was cast fresh off the success of the sleeper hit *The Warriors* (1979). Jeff Lynne of ELO, who had

just scored their biggest album to date, *Discovery*, was then asked to write half the film's soundtrack with Newton-John. Together, these combined efforts ballooned *Xanadu* to titanic proportions. In retrospect, such a massive production almost seems destined to fail.

And fail it did. Numerous rewrites left the script barely coherent, and many found the film tonally inconsistent (did we mention there's an animated sequence in which the leads turn into fish?). Universal Pictures lost faith in the picture before its advance screening and critics pelted it with negative reviews. It earned a mere $23 million, scarcely more than its $20 million budget. It was mocked so heavily that

Gene Kelly rolls in.

the infamous Golden Raspberry Awards (or Razzies) was created specifically for this and *Can't Stop the Music* (1980). *Xanadu* was nominated for Worst Picture at the First Annual Razzies, and Robert Greenwald won the Worst Director Award. While the film performed dismally, ELO and Newton-John clocked in another hit as the soundtrack did gangbusters on the Billboard charts.

Like some of the best movies unappreciated in their time, *Xanadu*'s failure didn't keep away new viewers for long. Over the years, the film has become a certified cult classic and one of the most beloved musicals of its age. Audiences in 1980 simply weren't ready

for *Xanadu*. It's possible that even 2020s film lovers aren't ready either, but mark our words, the day will come when this movie gets its proper accolades and will be seen as the underrated masterpiece it is. A Broadway musical version of *Xanadu* opened in 2009 and was celebrated with Tony Award nominations and Outer Circle Critics and Drama Desk Award wins, exposing new audiences to the infamous legacy of the film.

During these ever-changing and trying times, the world needs to find salvation in *Xanadu*. When you're feeling low and helpless and unable to escape the doom of online scrolling, do yourself a favor and escape into

the blindly bright, sunny, bubbly world of *Xanadu* and get reacquainted with your inner peace there. It will remind you that a new day is on the horizon and you're not alone because "All Over the World" others feel your pain. *Xanadu* tells us, "Don't Walk Away" from the fight, but stay engaged and aware. It will remind you "I'm Alive" and that we have to believe in "Magic." Through a slew of bizarre images, insane plot jumps, and among the wildest outfits ever seen on-screen (the film's costume designer, Bobbie Mannix, designed 260 costumes for *Xanadu*), it has the ability to transport us all to a "place where nobody dared to go" and can make us "open [our] eyes and see what we made is real, we are in Xanadu." If you watch this movie and aren't transported to that glorious place, it's okay. It just means the timing isn't right. But one day—one special, glorious day—you will find yourself in *Xanadu*, and when you're flocking through those heavenly fields of smoke machines and everlasting love, look for us roller-skating on the dance floor, blissed out in glory, and covered in a Day-Glo sheen.

OPPOSITE FROM TOP: Olivia Newton-John and a sea of legs • Michael Beck, Olivia Newton-John, and Gene Kelly

OMG Moment

Where does one start with *Xanadu*? Where does one end? Can a mere moment from this movie be encapsulated? Should one make sure they pay close attention to every detail of the "Dancin'" musical number, in which instruments and bodies are used to accentuate dance moves? Will you still audibly say "Oh my god!" when you actually *see* the animated sequence? Will the pure joy on Gene Kelly's face as he rolls around a skating rink in split screen not make your heart sigh "Oh my god"? Cowboys, tiger-print outfits, fashion shows, you name it, *Xanadu*'s got it. And all of it will make you say "OMG" for better or for worse.

THE PYRAMID

USA, 1976 • COLOR, 99 MINUTES

Michael Ashe as Phil

DIRECTOR: Gary Kent   **SCREENPLAY:** Gary Kent, Thomas J. Kelly
STARRING: Michael Ashe (Phil), Tomi Barrett (Merleen),
Charley Brown (Chris Lowe), June Christopher (Iris),
Ira Hawkins (Lemoine "LA" Peabody), Leonidas Ossetynski (Oracle)

In 1941, writer-director Preston Sturges made a charming and socially reflective comedic drama that is undoubtedly one of the best in his long line of outstanding work. *Sullivan's Travels* stars Joel McCrea as a rich and successful film director tired of making schlocky comedies for profit. Knowing that there's more to life that film can reflect, he embarks on a moneyless journey through America, looking for inspiration to capture the human condition on-screen. Along the way he meets a varied cast of characters while Veronica Lake serves as his traveling buddy as they experience the highs and lows afforded to those without capital. Fast forward nearly thirty years, and director Gary Kent made *The Pyramid*, his own version of this journey but in a manner all his own, not bound by studio expectations or unwritten rules against alienating viewers.

The Pyramid draws you in with its shocking opening scene that feels at once nostalgic and whimsical, only to turn the American dream into a tragic nightmare. The sensationalist aspect of kicking off the movie with a car crash does exactly what the filmmaker intends: it crushes any semblance of an expectation viewers may have about this film and launches it on its own journey. And *The Pyramid* is indeed a journey, a wild one that takes you on zigs and zags, over and under. At one point there's a ditch you must crawl through, and lots of climbing before you finally make it to bright, warm light at the end of the tunnel. At times *The Pyramid* feels less like a film and more like a video pamphlet enticing you into its world in cult fashion. *The Pyramid* doesn't follow the formula of *Sullivan's Travels* or any socially conscious picture made during the studio era but has all the familiar earmarks of one.

Mostly produced from the 1930s to the 1950s, but still undoubtedly part of the cinematic fabric of today, social pictures were films (usually made by an established director who could afford to lose money) intended to give the audience a message rather than just spectacle and entertainment. In *Sullivan's Travels* it's poverty, the human condition, and the power of comedy; in William Wellman's *Wild Boys of the Road*, it's about the abandoned children during the Great Depression. In *The Pyramid*, it's spiritual awakening and expanding one's consciousness.

Phil (Michael Ashe) and Lemoine "LA" Peabody (Ira Hawkins) are two Dallas news reporters striving to attain success in their jobs. LA

The Pyramid and its powerful effect

seeks outward perfectionism, attempting to move his way up in the media world, but off camera he's self-critical, emotionally despondent, violent, and depressed. Phil is also unhappy with his life and his job, as he is unable to find an audience for the stories he wants to tell. He's constantly criticized by his boss, who tells him that his pieces on human consciousness, suffering, and the negative effects of urbanization are sappy and unwanted. The two men struggle to find meaning in their lives with tragic results, but *The Pyramid* leaves room for a story that continues to grow more confident in the social message it delivers.

The Pyramid may sound dated, and its concept was not well received by the masses at the time of its release. But in this current Age of Aquarius, *The Pyramid* is ripe for rediscovery. Through Phil's news stories, we the audience are treated to numerous conversations about the nature of consciousness, the power

of magnetic healing, human energy fields and vibrations, and finding balance and harmony in the world. Phil starts the film frustrated, lonely, and bitter about his life, but as time progresses and he learns from the New Age movement and a therapist he starts seeing, he becomes more vocal about the possibility of changing the world from within. Much of the conversations happening throughout this film are reminiscent of wisdom shared by spiritual thinkers like Deepak Chopra, Eckhart Tolle, Marianne Williamson, and countless YouTubers and social media influencers who ascribe to magical thinking and the law of attraction.

The Pyramid captures the infancy of the modern-day New Age movement that began decades ago, and it reflects the American psyche as it underwent a major shift. The social upheaval and change created by various social revolutions in the 1960s took an interesting turn in the 1970s; the Vietnam War and the constant

FROM LEFT: Ira Hawkins stars as news reporter LA Peabody. • Newscaster Phil having a drag

fear of impending doom from the Cold War led to a rise in cults, as Americans began looking for deeper meaning in the changing tides and away from traditional practices.

Gary Kent isn't widely known for his work as a director, but he has been immortalized on-screen in Quentin Tarantino's *Once Upon a Time in Hollywood* (2019). An actor and stuntman with an illustrious career, Kent served as the inspiration for Brad Pitt's Oscar-winning performance as Clint Booth. Kent's work behind the camera is far less known, but he's proven himself a phenomenal filmmaker who keeps *The Pyramid* thrilling and unpredictable. His work is that of a sensitive artist, one who is more than competent in his visual style. There are some outstanding, gorgeous shots throughout *The Pyramid* reminding viewers that there's a visual poet behind the camera. *The Pyramid* is a hidden gem that's rough around the edges with its low-quality film stock that at times gives it a made-for-television look, but its rare form makes it worth appreciating. It's guaranteed to raise your vibrations.

Cult Connections

Director Gary Kent's laid-back, West Coast persona and riveting life experiences were crystallized in cinema by a relaxed, stoner-influenced performance from actor Brad Pitt in *Once Upon a Time in Hollywood* (2019). Pitt's cool factor, inspired by Kent, was so intoxicating to audiences and critics alike that it earned him his first Oscar win. Like his cinematic alter ego, Kent was a stunt double and actor, and his work can be seen in a number of a low-budget B films from the 1960s and '70s, including *Psych-Out* (1968), featuring Jack Nicholson before he broke into the mainstream; the Russ Tamblyn biker-spoliation drama *Satan's Sadists* (1969); and in *Bubba Ho-Tep* (2002), starring modern-day cult movie icon Bruce Campbell of *Evil Dead* fame.

THANK GOD IT'S FRIDAY

USA, 1978 • COLOR, 89 MINUTES

"Dancing! Everything else is bullshit."—Marv Gomez

DIRECTOR: Robert Klane   **SCREENPLAY:** Armyan Bernstein

STARRING: Valerie Landsburg (Frannie), Terri Nunn (Jeannie), Chick Vennera (Marv Gomez), Donna Summer (Nicole Sims), Ray Vitte (Bobby Speed), Mark Lonow (Dave), Andrea Howard (Sue), Jeff Goldblum (Tony Di Marco), Robin Menken (Maddy), Debra Winger (Jennifer), The Commodores (Themselves)

The mid-1970s ushered in a new style of upbeat music that first gained its popularity on the dance floors of New York clubs often frequented by Blacks, Latinos, and members of the LGBTQ community. As the '70s continued, this style of music—a pounding four-on-the-floor drum beat under electric pianos, rhythm guitars, and string synthesizers—broke out of small clubs and pulsated into the mainstream. With a largely disillusioned nation looking for a distraction from everyday life, the craze exploded, causing recording studios to add synthesizers, drum machines, and orchestral sections to their songs to stay relevant. The phenomenon included full-page magazine spreads and a breakout film called *Saturday Night Fever*, giving everyone from the boroughs of New York to small-town America a bout of disco fever.

Right after Rick Dees's chart-topping song "Disco Duck" broke into the Billboard Top 100 and just before the era's defining sound met its untimely (or timely, depending on your taste) demise at the 1979 Disco Demolition Night at Comiskey Park in Chicago, Columbia Pictures cemented its contribution to the musical craze with this 1978 musical comedy featuring Jeff Goldblum, the Commodores, and Donna Summer in her feature-film debut. Since Saturdays were off the table (thanks to John Badham's *Fever*), freshman director Robert Klane took the reins on spotlighting the next best day of the week on this picture produced by Motown Records and Casablanca Filmworks. Though it was critically panned upon its release, *Thank God It's Friday* was far from a box-office bomb, tripling profits on its $2.2 million budget.

This paper-thin story may not hold much weight, but what it lacks in depth, development, or even plot, it makes up for in humor and a funky spirit beckoning disco fans today who still anxiously await the return of the dance craze. It's Friday night and we meet a series of random people on their way to a popular Los Angeles nightclub. Some of them are regulars looking to hit the dance floor; some are just trying to win prize money from the night's dance competition; others are looking for love, some action; and one poor soul is just trying to find the damn place so that the Commodores can play as planned. We witness the mishaps and wacky antics taking place on the dance floor and in the bathrooms of the nightclub, all backed by the thumping sounds of the club DJ, while Donna Summer delights

FROM LEFT: The Commadores bring the house down. • Jeff Goldblum starts to boogie on the dance floor.

as a starry-eyed singer attempting to arrange her big break.

If it sounds like a lot, that's because it is. There's arguably too much going on as the ensemble cast is comprised of close to twenty patrons that we follow in this eighty-nine-minute feature. And while it's not enough of a runtime for most of the characters to make an impact, it's the right amount of time to keep your attention as it jumps back and forth and snakes around the club catching slice-of-life moments at the height of an iconic era. For time capsule reasons alone, *Thank God It's Friday* is a gem, capturing the pastel colors, impossibly-tight-yet-somehow-agile outfits, questionable haircuts, severely short hot pants, and enough hairspray to smell the Aqua Net through the screen. Goldblum gets the most screen time as the club's slimy owner who embarks on a nightly

bet with the DJ to bed a random clubber. On this particular night, the bet is on a square wife whose even squarer husband goes on a wild journey after he accidently takes a tidy sum of drugs at the club.

While Goldblum is a treat, standing tall enough to eclipse everyone while somehow making the leisure suit fad of the time look appealing, it's the performances that make this potentially forgettable flash in the pan a memorable joy. Summer is beyond charming, and the camera loves her. For a singer with no dramatic training, she possesses unexpectedly sharp timing, on display in the film's few random sketch comedy–like moments that ultimately lead to her climactic performance of "Last Dance"—Summer's chart-topping signature tune, which made its debut in this film and won the Oscar for Best Music, Original Song. When the performance

starts, it's surprisingly goose bumps–inducing. Taking the stage for an equally exciting performance are the Commodores, decked from head to toe in their late-1970s regalia of disco-ball-infused leatherwear that makes seeing them on a dance floor in their prime a most spectacular sight.

Donna Summer prepares to shine.

OMG Moment

The unexpected Gene Kelly–inspired dance solo that happens outside the club by leather-clad regular Marv Gomez (aka Leatherman) is a sight to behold. While outside taking a toke, he sees a lonely teen down on his luck. Worse yet, the kid can't dance (he proves this in a later scene when he just can't find the right beats to clap on). Leatherman gives the youngster a speedy lesson in the art of dance, which builds from an instruction to a full-blown number that includes flips on parked cars, tap-dancing on top of a phone booth, swinging from a light post, and acrobatics worthy of Olympic consideration—all while wearing a skintight brown leather outfit that moves with the dexterity of a second skin. It's a scene that feels completely out of place and ludicrous, but it's arguably the moment that makes the whole film. Leave it to Leatherman to deliver *Thank God It's Friday*'s most iconic line: "Dancing. Everything else is bullshit!"

BEYOND THE VALLEY OF THE DOLLS

USA, 1970 • COLOR, 109 MINUTES

Cynthia Myers, Marcia McBroom, and Dolly Read as the Carrie Nations

DIRECTOR: Russ Meyer   **SCREENPLAY:** Roger Ebert

STARRING: Dolly Read (Kelly MacNamara), Cynthia Myers (Casey Anderson),

Marcia McBroom (Petronella Danforth), John Lazar (Ronnie "Z-Man" Barzell),

Michael Blodgett (Lance Rocke)

An opening title card to the film *Beyond the Valley of the Dolls* reads, "The film you are about to see is not a sequel to *Valley of the Dolls*." While not an official follow-up to the 1967 film adaptation of Jacqueline Susann's best-selling novel, there are some interesting similarities: the trio of women at the forefront, the story about Hollywood newbies, corrupt industry types, and, of course, those "downer" prescription pills called "dolls." But while *Valley of the Dolls* was a straight classic drama starring famous actresses such as Patty Duke and Susan Hayward, *Beyond the Valley of the Dolls* was a satire made by true outsiders who could only depict an approximation of Tinseltown. Director Russ Meyer had until this time spent his career outside Hollywood, first making industrial films after his stint in World War II, and then shooting centerfolds for *Playboy* magazine. He began making his own independent films in the 1950s that featured copious amounts of nudity, eventually becoming known for his signature formula: the exploits of powerful, big-breasted women. Fox studio president Richard Zanuck invited Meyer to direct *Beyond the Valley of the Dolls* based on a 1968 film Meyer had produced and directed called *Vixen*, which had cost relatively little to make (roughly $70,000) but grossed more than six times that amount. Zanuck, impressed with the feat, had experienced a series of box-office failures and was desperate to connect with a younger audience. Meyer tapped friend and film critic Roger Ebert to write the movie; it was his very first time penning a screenplay. Meyer refused to hire studio-suggested talent and instead

gathered the people he knew from his world: ex-*Playboy* centerfolds Dolly Read and Cynthia Myers, the star of *Vixen*, Erica Gavin, and others that he believed perfect for the parts. The resulting film is a dizzying cross-genre showcase, a rock-and-roll-musical–meets-comedy satire, melodrama, and gore film all at once. A sensory delight on every level, *Beyond the Valley of the Dolls* is like an episode of *The Monkees* with boobs. The

Director Russ Meyer stages a hot tub scene.

The band performs.

sheer combustion of varied story elements is awe-inspiring; in a world where sudden medical miracles happen alongside grisly murders, barely clothed women are running the show as the men fight in their wake, all ending with a voice-of-God narrator telling everyone to just love one another.

The film centers around the Kelly Affair, an all-girl band reminiscent of Josie and the Pussycats, composed of lead singer Kelly MacNamara (Dolly Read), bass player Casey Anderson (Cynthia Myers), and drummer

Petronella Danforth (Marcia McBroom). Alongside their manager (and Kelly's beau) Harris Allsworth (David Gurian), they perform at a high school prom and promptly decide to travel to California to meet Kelly's aunt, fashion industry ad woman Susan Lake (Phyllis Davis). Kelly learns that Susan got a hefty family inheritance that she is happy to share with her niece, but her lawyer, Porter Hall (Duncan McLeod), tries to convince her that Kelly and her hippie friends are only after her money. Susan invites the band to a party hosted by the ultimate king of the scene, Ronnie "Z-Man" Barzell (John Lazar). A rock-and-roll "it" man, he is equal parts Phil Spector and Shakespearean protagonist. Z-Man is theatrical, has an affinity for all things royal, and his castle is filled with a wide assortment of partygoers who are either having sex, doing drugs, or both. As Z-Man holds court, he introduces Kelly to the cast of characters in attendance while real-life musical group Strawberry Alarm Clock rocks the dance floor. Fascinatingly, the crowd is filled with people of all ages, races, and sexual and gender identities, everyone conversing in slightly over-the-top 1960s hipster slang. Z-Man exclaims, "This is my happening and it freaks me out!" while Kelly replies, "Oh, it's a stone gas, man!" The viewer can't help but agree.

The Kelly Affair eventually performs their song "Sweet Talking Candy Man" at the party while Kelly seductively works the crowd. Their music impresses Z-Man so much that he adopts them as his new project, renames them the Carrie Nations, and immediately launches their big music careers. Kelly is soon courted by Hollywood hunk (and notorious gold digger) Lance Rocke (Michael Blodgett), whose perfect blond and muscled physique just happens to also be the obsession of Z-Man. Meanwhile, Kelly's former flame, Harris, is left dumped and bewildered, with the hilariously oversexed porn star Ashley St. Ives (Edy Williams) trying to grab his attention. Harris is so bereft that he ends up succumbing to drug addiction, a passion that he shares with the dissociated Casey, who downs the dolls on a regular basis.

Petronella, on the other hand, has a meet-cute with party waiter (and law student) Emerson Thorne (Harrison Page), beginning a sweet relationship that plays in gorgeous contrast to the others in the film but isn't totally without drama; heavyweight boxer Randy Black (James Iglehart) attempts to horn in on their happiness.

The Carrie Nations are on the fast track, yet somehow, even more turbulence is in store for them as the movie plays on. Russ Meyer was known to love what he called "express-train pacing," and Beyond the Valley of the Dolls might be one of the fastest-cut movies on record. Add to this the colorful costumes and hippie ephemera, and this cult classic functions as its own acid trip.

Did You Know

The music performed by the Kelly Affair/ the Carrie Nations is only lip-synced by the actresses. Kelly MacNamara's lead vocals were provided by Lynn Carey, lead singer of the '60s psychedelic blues group Mama Lion. Barbara Robison, lead singer of the psych-pop band the Peanut Butter Conspiracy, also provided vocals for the songs in the film. Composer Stu Phillips wrote the band's songs for the film and has provided the music for several classic cult movies and TV shows throughout the years, including *Hells Angels on Wheels*, *The Gay Deceivers*, *Macon County Line*, *Battlestar Galactica*, and *The Monkees*.

HEAD

USA, 1968 • COLOR, 86 MINUTES

The Monkees attempt to swim to freedom.

DIRECTOR: Bob Rafelson   **SCREENPLAY:** Bob Rafelson, Jack Nicholson
STARRING: Micky Dolenz (uncredited), Davy Jones (uncredited), Michael Nesmith (uncredited), Peter Tork, Annette Funicello (Minnie), Timothy Carey (Lord High 'n Low), Logan Ramsey (Off. Faye Lapid), Abraham Sofaer (Swami)

In 1968, the Beatles had a hold on the music scene with numerous chart-topping albums under their belt, two successful musical feature films (and a third one on the way), and enough innovative greatness that their legacy is still touted over fifty years after their breakup. Across the pond in America, the Monkees were living in the shadows of the band they were often compared to but managed to find success in an area the Beatles had not: television. The Monkees, consisting of members Peter Tork, Mike Nesmith, Davy Jones, and Micky Dolenz, had been inspired by the Beatles' *A Hard Day's Night* (1964) and were formed to be a parody group for a television series by New York producers Bob Rafelson and Bert Schneider.

The group became an unexpected smash recording act, especially among younger fans, thanks to their quirky series, *The Monkees*, that often placed the men in wacky situations that they had to get out of. The series won an Emmy award, and the group made four albums during the show's reign. But the Monkees were pelted with criticism that they weren't legitimate musicians because their albums often involved session players instead of them on actual instruments, even though each member was a professionally skilled musician. (Dolenz was the only Monkee who had to learn to play an instrument for the camera.) The comparisons to the Beatles went from being a fun jest by critics to a frustrating box that the men felt stuck in for most of their time in the spotlight. That box became the theme of their 1968 film *Head*. Written by Rafelson and then screenwriter and struggling actor Jack Nicholson, *Head* is a stream-of-consciousness film that's just as self-aware as it is strange.

The Monkees star as themselves, or rather versions of themselves trapped in the image of the Monkees. *Head* is a meta story without a true end or beginning that ties a series of skits and musical performances together. They narrate the film's purpose, or lack thereof, in its "Theme Song," stating, "You say we're manufactured, to that we all agree. So make your choice and we'll rejoice in never being free. Hey, hey we are the Monkees, we've said it all before. The money's in we're made of tin, we're here to give you more!" The film immediately shifts from its quirky, humorous vibe to a scream placed over news footage of Vietnam general Nguyễn Ngọc Loan executing Viet Cong officer Nguyễn Văn Lém. The scream is then revealed to be for the Monkees as they take the stage

Davy Jones, Peter Tork, Micky Dolenz, and Mike Nesmith soak up sun in the desert.

to perform. This sequence establishes the film's modus operandi as a critique of pop culture and political state of affairs in 1968.

Rafelson was on the way to becoming a keen figure in the counterculture film scene, which would allow him to break into the mainstream in 1970 after his follow-up feature starring Jack Nicholson, *Five Easy Pieces* (1970). But in 1968, Rafelson only had *Head* and a few episodes of *The Monkees* in his directing arsenal; consequently, the film feels like a playground for the director to find his voice and vision. It possesses brilliant moments of editing and special effects, allowing Rafelson's vision to be clear and precise, and making the film bold, funny, and poignant. *Head* marks one of the first times the process of solarization was used in film to manipulate the color and contrast of an image in psychedelic ways. These radical processes give the Monkees a sturdy soapbox on which to stand up to critics and make known their own viewpoints away from their squeaky-clean image.

During one scene in particular, Peter punches a waitress in drag and someone yells "cut." In meta fashion, Rafelson and Nicholson appear on-screen in front of the camera to prepare for the next shot. Peter expresses his concern with hitting a woman and asks his bandmates and Rafelson to think about the message it'll send to the kids. The notions of message and image are constantly brought up, including a scene in which singer Frank Zappa appears in a cameo as himself. After watching Davy Jones perform a musical break, Frank tells Jones that his song was pretty "white" and that he should work on his musical skills because people look up to him. Such humorous moments make up some of the film's best comic sequences. But all wasn't rosy on the set of *Head*.

Rafelson had become disillusioned by the Monkees as a project. The series had been canceled after its second season in 1967. Together, Rafelson and Nicholson sought to effectively end the Monkees with their daring script for *Head*. The two gathered ideas for the script during marijuana-laced brainstorm sessions recorded by tape player, and Nicholson finalized the script while on an LSD trip. On top of this, while the Monkees were battling Columbia records over their salaries and contracts, they learned that Rafelson would not credit them as writers on the film. This caused Micky, Davy, and Mike to boycott shooting on the first day of filming. The project continued to be marred by personal and professional restraints, which made the film's epic box-office failure a final, fatal blow for the group.

As it turned out, the fans that looked up to the Monkees were too young to latch onto a satirical film with anti-capitalism and anti-war sentiments. It didn't help that the movie was poorly marketed in a guerilla-style tactic on the streets of New York and publicized with promotional material that didn't even show the band. When the film flopped, it effectively cut ties between the Monkees and Rafelson. Tork left the band after *Head* and bought out his contract, effectively ending his tenure with the Monkees. The band released three more albums after the soundtrack for *Head*, all without Peter and the final without Mike. The band reunited on and off throughout the years, and *Head* eventually went on to find its place with cult-movie status, receiving praise from a new audience decades later. Its trippy, surreal story mixed with its ability to be an eye-opening time capsule of pop culture and the brief but mighty reign of the Monkees makes it a film that's worthy of recognition. In a long-delayed happy ending, the band and Nicholson all commented fondly about the film in later years, admitting pride in how it turned out.

Davy Jones dances with Toni Basil.

Did You Know

Choreographer and one-hit wonder Toni Basil of "Mickey" fame appears in *Head* as a dancer alongside Davy Jones in the performance "Daddy's Song," which she choreographed. Another interesting tidbit is Mike Nesmith's creation of MTV, on which Basil's song played and helped skyrocket her to success. When making a promotional video for his 1977 single "Rio," Nesmith decided to make the video a comedic short with his music over it. This idea led him to put together a pilot that including videojocks, or VJs, as they would become known, who hosted these music videos. Nesmith took the idea to Warner Bros. where they partnered with American Express and turned the concept into the MTV network, launched in 1981. Nesmith was offered a position as the network's head, but he turned it down to pursue other creative endeavors.

THE TRIP

USA, 1967 • COLOR, 82 MINUTES

Hippies enjoying a Happening

DIRECTOR: Roger Corman **SCREENPLAY:** Jack Nicholson

STARRING: Peter Fonda (Paul Groves), Susan Strasberg (Sally Groves),

Bruce Dern (John), Dennis Hopper (Max), Salli Sachse (Glenn),

Barboura Morris (Flo), Dick Miller (Cash)

The year 1967 is almost as synonymous with LSD as the year 2000 is with the Y2K scare. A generation of young Baby Boomers born in the 1940s and '50s were looking for answers to life's deepest quandaries through strips of paper blotted with Lysergic acid diethylamide ("acid" for short); they were also speeding up societal change. In the process, everything in popular culture—from music and movies to politics and social movements—became tie-dyed and laden with flowers. This cohort of teens and young adults, aptly known as hippies, flocked to California during the "Summer of Love" in 1967, beckoned by the promise of a new world. Most of these teens were simply aware that something different was in the air and they wanted to be a part of it, to separate themselves from their parents' generation. Others were attempting to find the meaning of life in casual sex, drug use, and an experimental way of living that meant free clothes, food, and aid for all who needed it.

During this social transformation, the art world began to reflect the cultural shift at a breakneck pace. The Beatles grew their hair longer and openly experimented with acid, the Beach Boys turned from surfer dudes into introspective visionaries, clothes became brightly patterned, and American cinema saw the birth of its own New Wave, also known as New Hollywood, a catch-all term for movies produced outside the stronghold of Hollywood's once powerful but now crumbling studio system. In the midst of this New Wave, the son of classic Hollywood star Henry Fonda, Peter, became one of the key faces of that change and its rippling effects. In 1969,

Peter would go on to make the revolutionary, groundbreaking counterculture film *Easy Rider*. But two years prior, he starred in producer Roger Corman's *The Trip*, a film that perfectly captures the essence of 1967.

Fonda made his first collaboration with the influential Corman in the 1966 film *The Wild Angels*. Corman, a master of genre and exploitation films of his era, based the film around the popular Hells Angels motorcycle gang. Following the trend of spotlighting the newest and hippest movements of his time, Corman teamed up with then struggling actor and screenwriter Jack Nicholson for a treatment about an uptight producer looking to break free of his hesitation and setbacks. Together they made *The Trip*, casting Fonda, who had already developed a reputation as a "dropout," or stoner and heavy drug user in the L.A. scene.

With the combined efforts of a group of white male stoners gallivanting around Hollywood, the group, which also included fellow actor and dropout Dennis Hopper, was able to make an incredible visual juggernaut that used innovative practical effects to capture the mind-blowing results of "tripping" under the influence of LSD. These influential visuals would populate mainstream media for years to come, most notably the pot circle in the television series *That '70s Show*, the melting floors and shifting perspectives in Terry Gilliam's *Fear and Loathing in Las Vegas*, and a slew of other on-screen psychedelic sequences, cementing its status as a cinematic forerunner.

The Trip is simple in its delivery but manages to be a complex and profound journey in its

FROM LEFT: Paul Groves (Peter Fonda) coming up on an acid trip • A groovy dance party in *The Trip*

brief eighty-two-minute runtime. Fonda stars as Paul Groves, a television producer feeling lost and alienated after his wife divorces him. With a little help from his friends, he gets high and is convinced to take a deeper look at his feelings by turning on, tuning in, and dropping out. He's given a hit of acid and begins an existential journey in which he is confronted with his fears, his hopes, his illusions, and the real world. Things get trippy and weird, as they only can when dosed, and a number of guides come in and out of his trip before he breaks on through to the other side.

The Trip is obviously and cautiously pro-LSD, unlike its 1968 counterpart *Pysch-Out*, an antidrug parable in which Bruce Dern, Susan Strasberg, and Nicholson are also involved. *The Trip* paints the experience of tripping in a mostly positive light. Although it doesn't shy away from the negative and frightening aspects of LSD, unlike many movies about the effects of drugs, *The Trip* acts as a guide of sorts for anyone who chooses to partake. It shows the good, the bad, and the ugly in authentically creative ways using body paint, an array of varying lights, shadows, and in-camera editing to showcase the effects of the drug throughout the character's trip. Much of the reason for this authenticity is due in large part to

Paul Groves goes into a deeper trip.

Corman and his crew being under the influence of LSD while filming.

The Trip was a success upon its release, both in terms of profit and in its lasting influence on the careers of Fonda, Nicholson, Dern, and Strasberg. It sparked an ample amount of drug pictures that followed in its path, leading to the film becoming virtually lost at sea in a litany of psychedelic-inspired counterparts. Nevertheless, its place as a forerunner and personification of its time period makes it a cultural staple that will be viewed for decades to come as a psychedelic summer-of-love encapsulation that is so spot on, it almost feels like parody.

Cult Connections

Talk about a who's who of cult cinema in the 1960s and '70s! This movie has so many random cult movie connections that its title alone could probably aid in any game of Six Degrees of Separation. Actress Luana Anders's cult connections include her turn in *Night Tide*, Francis Ford Coppola's early horror film *Dementia 13*, and Fonda's directorial debut, *Easy Rider*. Actor Dick Miller is featured and is primarily known for his starring role in the cult horror film *A Bucket of Blood* (1959) and as one of Roger Corman's stock actors. Also featured is Bruce Dern, star of the cult sci-fi film *Silent Running* (1972); Barboura Morris of *The Wasp Woman* (1959); and Dennis Hopper, who also starred in *Night Tide* and *Easy Rider* and should always be top of mind when playing Six Degrees thanks to an illustrious and expansive career. The man will get you anywhere you need to go in the game!

FUNERAL PARADE OF ROSES

JAPAN, 1969 • B&W, 105 MINUTES

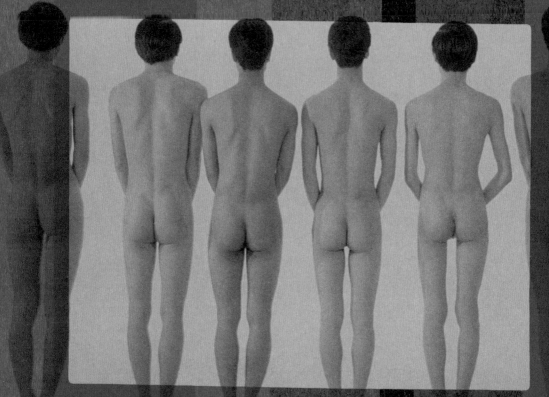

A special present from the boys

DIRECTOR: Toshio Matsumoto **SCREENPLAY:** Toshio Matsumoto

STARRING: Pītā (Eddie), Osamu Ogasawara (Leda), Yoshimi Jō (Jimi),

Koichi Nakamura (Juju), Flamenco Umeji (Greco), Saako Oota (Mari),

Tarō Manji (Nora), Toyosaburo Uchiyama (Guevara)

"All definitions of cinema have been erased; all doors are open now." Attributed to Lithuanian-born filmmaker Jonas Mekas, this line is quoted by a student in *Funeral Parade of Roses* after a series of loosely connected scenes have aggressively zipped past on-screen, setting these words into clear meaning by the time we hear them. During those whirling twenty minutes, what we are shown are scenes that haven't yet come to fruition in the film: protests, a murder, a memory of a lead character's childhood trauma, a cabaret show, and a documentary-style interview. All these shots are tied together through quick edits, connecting the moments into a slightly coherent kaleidoscope before its focus snaps back to the group of students watching what we are led to believe is a cut of *Funeral Parade of Roses*. We are reminded that they started this viewing party after a drunken, marijuana-fueled party that ended in LSD being passed around. As if we, the audience, are also emerging from a drug-induced haze, we're left wondering how much of that was the students' experience and how much was meant to be ours?

This mind-bending cinematic play is just the first act of a jarring, surrealist drama centered on a group of predominately gay, trans, and queer youths going about their day-to-day lives in Japan. What makes their story so fascinating is the Greek-tragedy inspired tale at the core of it. Eddie (Pītā) is a transgender female vying for the opportunity to be the Queen in charge of a local gay establishment. Her rising place among the ranks and in the eyes of a drug-dealing businessman, Jimi, makes Eddie the natural enemy of Leda, who owns the bar

and is Jimi's lover. Inevitably, pride and jealously get in the way and Eddie finds herself in the middle of an *Oedipus Rex* retelling.

That's just the basic plot. In between and all around this plot is a series of interviews, portions of dialogue, scenes of partying, and moments of social protest that reminds viewers of the political unrest happening all over the world in the 1960s. Director Toshio Matsumoto wasn't afraid to experiment with letting the past and present collide in his film, mixing an ageless, tragic story with the bourgeoning openly queer subculture of Japan's underground. Made at the height of a number of the New Wave movements happening around the world, such as French, Brazilian,

The ladies of the club

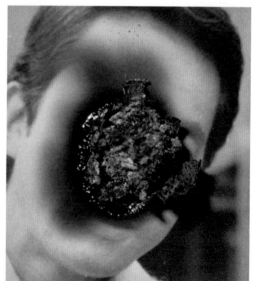

CLOCKWISE FROM TOP: Appearances aren't what they seem. •
The burned image of fate • Eddie (Pītā) showers.

and Czech, Matsumoto's film feels like an open dialogue with his contemporaries Jean-Luc Godard, Miloš Forman, Věra Chytilová, and Glauber Rocha. *Funeral Parade of Roses* highlights the cultural, cinematic, and icon-oclastic shifts happening in post-war Japan. The film breathes with freshness, thanks to Matsumoto's stunning visuals.

Matsumoto makes a film that's both tender and challenging, weaving together intimate close-ups and camera angles that sometimes grace the faces of real-life onlookers from the streets watching the process of the film being made. Toshie Iwasa's edits are sharp, precise, and poignant reminders of how simply powerful editing can be. The meaning that is imbued by quick flashes here and pauses there or jump cuts from one scene to another and back again is impressive. During one sequence, the camera follows a dazed and melancholy Eddie down a street before cutting to a different time on a different street: now the camera shows Eddie's POV when confronted by a group of men who follow in front, jeering for attention. Another cut reveals Eddie walking away from the men before running into a delivery boy. The scene frantically cuts back and forth before a stranger approaches and propositions Eddie. She runs off, attempting escape, and we get more quick cuts of Eddie being leered at, chased, and watched by someone. At times other men. At times the camera itself. The scene is haunting in its ability to capture the fear of being scrutinized as a minority.

Although this marked Matsumoto's feature-length debut, he was no stranger to film. He had made a number of documentaries and experimental shorts before *Funeral Parade of Roses*; some footage from those works is used in this film. He continued on with a lengthy career as a video artist and avant-garde filmmaker. The dazzling star Peter/Pītā made his debut here, then went on to a successful career in Japan as an actor and entertainer, appearing in Akira Kurosawa's *Ran*

(1985) and a number of television shows and video games. *Funeral Parade of Roses*'s influence lives on, not only for its own impressive innovations, but for inspiring future movies, reportedly even Stanley Kubrick's *A Clockwork Orange* (1971), specifically the sped-up threesome scene.

Genre-ly Speaking

The 1960s were a hotbed of creativity and social change all around the world. Many countries saw a shift in the kind of films being made as new, emerging filmmakers around the world were gaining access to movie equipment and sought to represent marginalized communities on-screen and interrogate the status quo, sparking New Wave movements that broke out worldwide. Some other standout films from various countries that were part of the New Wave movement in the late 1960s include

Glauber Rocha's Cinema Novo Brazilian film *Black God, White Devil* (1964)

Mikhail Kalatozov's Russian/Cuban production *I Am Cuba* (1964)

Věra Chytilová's Czechoslovakian film *Daisies* (1966)

Ousmane Sembene's Senegalese/French film *Black Girl* (1966)

Jean-Luc Godard's *Week-end* (1967)

INDEX

Note: Page references in *italics* indicate photographs.

ACKNOWLEDGMENTS

From MILLIE DE CHIRICO:

Writing a book around TCM Underground is something I thought would never happen, let alone during a pandemic, from two different countries! Thank you to my coauthor Toyiah Murry for agreeing to go on this ride together. Cult movies need people like you—thank you for your perspective and hard work!

A big thanks to our editor, Cindy Sipala, and everyone at Running Press. Thank you, Eileen Flanagan, for the tireless photo research.

I appreciate everyone at TCM who gave us the opportunity to write this book, including Pola Changnon, Genevieve McGillicuddy, Heather Margolis, and John Malahy. Thanks to Susana Zepeda, Liz Winter, Susan Biesack, Taryn Jacobs, Wendy Gardner, Justin Gottlieb, Diana Bosch, Scott McGee, and Alison Firor for their kind assistance during this process as well.

A huge thank you to Charlie Tabesh and Stephanie Thames in TCM Programming for their support of the franchise. I very much appreciate your trust in me throughout the years.

Many thanks to everyone at the network and beyond who championed and contributed to Underground, including Tim Reilly, Sean Cameron, Andrew Alonso, Josh Lubin, Jeff Stafford, John Miller, Richard Harland Smith, Stina Chyn, Alexa Foreman, David Byrne, Brandon Arnold, Katie Daniels, Julie Bitton, Melissa Yocom, John Nowak, Dori Stegman, Taryn Coleman, Yacov Freedman, John Renaud, and Hemrani Vyas.

Thanks to the fine folks at Videodrome and the Plaza Theater in Atlanta, Georgia, for their support.

To the TCM Slumberground crew (Ben Cheaves, Matthew Ownby, Jacob Griswell, and Bailey Tyler), thank you for your passion, creativity, and free time. Your dedication to this franchise never goes unnoticed by me!

I appreciate the kind support and advice of my family, friends, and those who lovingly came into my orbit while I was (often, frantically!) working on this project, including Danielle Henderson, Kurt Fausset, Vanessa Palacios, Heather Jewett, Christopher Schelling, Drennen Quinn, Taylor Burton, and Scott Jackson.

And finally, my endless gratitude to Eric Weber for coming up with the original idea and inspiration for TCM Underground.

From QUATOYIAH MURRY:

I'm still in awe that in the midst of a global pandemic, a move to a new continent, returning to university after a decade, and having my whole world tossed upside down that I managed to write a book about a some of my all-time favorite movies that are near and dear to my heart. It's been a dream come true that wouldn't have possible without a number of wonderful people.

I'd like to thank executive editor Cindy Sipala and the whole Running Press team for their professionalism and hard work at guiding us in giving these films another chance at appreciation through this fun, gorgeous book that I'm proud to be a part of. This includes our publisher Kristin Kiser, editors, designer Susan Van Horn, publicists, marketers, production staff, and sales force.

A big thank you to the amazing folks at TCM who continue to keep the greatest network on television compelling and comforting to watch. Thank you to Charlie Tabesh, John Malahy, Liz Winters, Susan Biesack, Heather Margolis, Eileen Flanagan, Pola Chagnon, and Genevieve McGillicuddy for being involved in the greenlighting of this concept and its creation. Also, thanks to Susana Zepeda, Dori Stegman, Taryn Jacobs, and Wendy Gardner. I'm grateful that we're now bonded by ink forever!

I'd also love to extend thank-yous to Justin Gottlieb, Diana Bosch, Marci Sacco, Dexter Fedor, Caroline Wigmore, Nicole Hill, Katie Daniels, Jacob Griswell, Jeanette Gregory, Allison Firor, Gordon Gyor, Ben Cheaves, Matthew Ownby, Hemrani Vyas, Taryn Coleman, Yacov Freedman, Julie Bitton, John Renaud, and Bailey Tyler for all of your support. Thank you also to Joshua Lubin, Andrew Alonso, Kristen Welch, Steve Denker, Christina Chyn, Shannon Clute, Donald Bogle, and Jacqueline Stewart.

I give my biggest thank you to Millie De Chirico for being my writing partner-in-crime and presenting me with this wonderful opportunity. I still remember being a starry-eyed new hire at TCM, completely incredulous to the fact that I got to work on promoting TCM Underground. I would have never imagined that I would have received the opportunity to program a few nights, manage a few theater screenings, and have a hand at creating its YouTube series counterpart *TCM Slumberground*. What a journey that's been! It's an honor to add being coauthor alongside you to the list of unreal things I've been able to do.

A special shout out to Videodrome Atlanta and all of its fantastic workers who make being a movie nerd feel cool. Plus, they've always helped me find whatever film I've ever needed. Likewise, a shoutout to Plaza Theatre for supporting my silly dreams of having silly TCM Underground–related screenings there.

And my sincerest love and thank you to all of the fantastic directors, artists, and crew members who made these movies that we love so much. From the first time I watched *Trolls 2* with my older brother, I knew I wanted more weird, offbeat movies in my life. Watching these types of movies with friends and family (and sometimes alone) over the years has been special and soul-affirming. I can't wait to continue being shaken and moved by the future gems that other creative, passionate artists of the future will make.